E.B. Wheatley Balme, Henry M Fletcher

Is the Use of the Vestments Under the Ornaments Rubric

Part of the Discipline Which the Church has Received?

E.B. Wheatley Balme, Henry M Fletcher

Is the Use of the Vestments Under the Ornaments Rubric
Part of the Discipline Which the Church has Received?

ISBN/EAN: 9783337000783

Printed in Europe, USA, Canada, Australia, Japan

Cover: Foto ©ninafisch / pixelio.de

More available books at **www.hansebooks.com**

IS THE USE OF THE

VESTMENTS

UNDER THE

ORNAMENTS RUBRIC

part of the Discipline which this

CHURCH

has received?

LETTERS BETWEEN THE
Rev. HENRY M. FLETCHER, M.A.
RECTOR OF GRASMERE

AND

E. B. WHEATLEY BALME, M.A.

RIVINGTONS
WATERLOO PLACE, LONDON
MDCCCLXXXIII

PREFACE.

The occasion of the following letters appears on the face of them. In sending them to the press, I have but to express my thanks to my excellent friend Mr. Fletcher for kindly criticism from his point of view; and for allowing me to print his letter (though not written with a view to publication) along with my own.

E. B. WHEATLEY BALME.

Cotewall, Mirfield,
    Ascensiontide, 1883.

TABLE OF CONTENTS.

	PAGE
FIRST LETTER TO MR. FLETCHER	1–6
MR. FLETCHER'S LETTER	7–14
SECOND LETTER TO MR. FLETCHER	15

§ I. *Absence of Evidence for Use of the Vestments.*

Mr. James Parker negatives use of vestments before 1566 ...	16
Inventories at All Saints, Derby	17
No vestments in Cecil's list of varieties, 1564–5 ...	18
Change of view in Cosin's "Notes" ...	19, 20
Present attitude of English Church Union	21
Vestments not used in Burleigh's chapel ...	22
Their use unknown to Convocation of 1562	23
Zurich Letters refer only to cope and surplice, with one possible exception proving the rule	24–26
Use of vestments unknown to Sandys in 1560	27
Contemporary silence as to the Rubric ...	28

§ II. *The Advertisements.*

Theory of a maximum and a minimum, modern ...	29
Sandys' gloss on the proviso as to ornaments	30
Elizabeth's Rubric from the first a dead letter till the recent metamorphosis	31, 32
The Queen scolds the Bishops for suffering diversities	33
Her own edicts contradicted each other	34
The Bishops' "Interpretations and further considerations"	35
They modified both Rubrics and Injunctions, effecting a compromise between contradictory edicts	36–39
Compromise accepted by the Queen, but not law	40

	PAGE
Uniformity to be evolved from chaos	41
To this end, the Archbishop drafts Ordinances	42
The Queen's motives for hesitation	43
Archbishop resolved to wait for her authority	44
Nothing done till disorders intolerable	45
The Archbishop called to the Queen's presence	46
The Archbishop gets her authority to " see good orders decreed "	47
"Order taken" in the Advertisements	48
Mr. Parker's theory antecedently improbable	49
Queen piloting the ship at her will	50
The Archbishop had no legislative authority of his own	51
Mr. Parker interprets Grindal's letter enclosing the Advertisements, typographically	52, 53
No authority in the MS. for Mr. Parker's typography	54
Testimony of Sampson and Humphrey	55
S. and H. attribute royal authority to the Advertisements	56
Mr. Parker's own admission	57
The Queen's policy at the time	58
Mr. Parker not a lawyer	59

§ III. *Authorized Destruction of Vestments.*

Royal Commissioners in Lincoln Diocese class vestments with *delenda*	60, 61
Copes still to be retained	62
The Injunctions modified by the Interpretations	63
Bullingham's position	64
Character and acts of Aylmer	65
If vestments legal, Aylmer doubly a law-breaker	66
Difference between the Interpretations and the Advertisements	67
Archbishop Grindal's York Injunctions, 1571, not explicable by mere puritanism	68, 69
Grindal's Injunctions in accordance with the law, or in defiance of both Queen and law	70, 71
The thing not done in a corner	72
Grindal's timid caution to the Canons, and refusal to go upon uncertainties, prove his mind clear as to the validity of the Advertisements	73–75
The Queen's marked approval of Grindal	76
Inquiry for vestments, etc., continued by others, Bishops and Royal Commissioners in both provinces	77, 78
Last traces, and final disappearance of vestments	79
History of vestments unintelligible unless other order was taken under Elizabeth	80, 81
Destruction the most effectual negative order	82

§ IV. *Canons of 1604.*

	PAGE
If the Rubric was still in force as to vestments, the 11th Canon of 1604-5 leads *ad absurdum* ...	83, 84
Supposition inconsistent with the 58th Canon	85
Attempts at reconciliation fail ...	86
The 58th Canon taken verbally from the Advertisements	87
Canon 24 expressly based on them	88
Rule of apparel received by the Church	89

§ V. *The Vestments at Durham.*

Cosin admitted the vestments to be not according to the Canons and Constitution of the Church ...	90, 91

§ VI. *Convocation of* A.D. 1661.

Verbal alterations in the Rubric, 1661 ...	92
How shown in facsimile of MS. ...	93
Omission of reference to the Act explained in Cosin's and Sancroft's MS. copies ...	94, 95
The words of the Act more exactly followed ...	96
The authority of Parliament admitted by the Rubric	97
Church authority ignored in Act 2 and 3 Ed. VI. c. 1	98
Preamble of the Act ...	99
Parliament judging on "prayers, rites, etc."	100
Clergy to be tried like trespassers ...	101
Spiritual jurisdiction "by virtue of the Act"	102
Like procedure under Elizabeth's Act and Rubric	103
Was the purpose of Convocation of 1661, entire change ?	104
Rubric made less imperative ...	105
But if Convocation intended diversity, it deceived Parliament	106, 107
The word "retained" then inserted in the Rubric, inapplicable to ornaments then non-existent	108, 109
Only existing ornaments could be retained ...	110
All times of ministrations made homogeneous ...	111
All the alterations tended to maintain the *status quo* ...	112
Convocations of 1604-5 accepted the Rubric only as modified by the Advertisements ...	113, 114
Bill for Uniformity passed Commons, July 9, 1661 ...	115
Cosin's "corrected copy" probably embodied results of consultations on revision, during the vacation ...	116, 117
Rapid revision of Ornaments Rubric	118

Table of Contents.

	PAGE
Letters to York from the king, and from all the bishops of the province	119, 120
Convocation consisting of three members, create, by return of post, plenipotentiaries for the whole clerus of the northern province	121-123
Rubric, as revised, unseen by northern clergy till fixed in the Prayer-book	124, 125
Synodical perplexity about the form of subscription	126, 127
What is "canonical obedience"?	128
Full and deliberate synodical action in 1604-5	129
Canons of 1604-5 now often ignored, in favour of Rubric standing on secular sanctions	130, 131
Confusion between "things which are God's, and things which are Cæsar's"	132, 133
Ornaments Rubric specially stamped as Cæsar's	134
Purpose of the Convocation of 1661, as to Rubric	135
King's warrant for the Savoy Conference	136
Exceptions of the Ministers	137
The Bishops' reasons for retaining the Rubric	138
If they intended to bring back vestments, they said what was not true	139, 140
Of the eight revisers, six were at the Savoy	141
Cosin never published his "Notes"	142
His visitation articles as Archdeacon	143
Cosin's part at the Savoy	144
Cosin deputed by Convocation to draft articles	145
His articles followed by seventeen bishops in 1662, requiring surplice for all times of ministration	146, 147
Rarity, in 1662, of First Book of Edward VI.	148
Bishop Morley's Articles, 1662, and Archbishop Sancroft's, 1686	149
Sancroft's special knowledge of the Convocation of 1661	150
No vestments in Cosin's private chapels	151
Did the Clerus of Convocation of 1661, use vestments?	152
Early negative evidence from "Admonition to Parliament"	153
Later negative from "Hierurgia Anglicana"	154
Were inconsistent standards raised in 1661?	155
Why is rubric on position of Holy Table disregarded?	156
Were burdens imposed which were not touched by the imposers?	157
African tailors' casula, *temp.* St. Augustine	158
Chasuble of modern type, "such as may now be seen in ritualistic churches," worn by a bridegroom of the 8th or 9th century	159-161
Chasuble first a sacerdotal dress in the darkest age	162
Surplice and stole most primitive	163
Primitive sacerdotal dress, white	164
Dr. Rock's admiration of the "old English surplice"	165

Table of Contents.

Appendix I.

Three names superscribed on the frontispiece; three martyr saints thus depicted by Pontiff contemporary with Third General Council ... 167-169

Appendix II.

Rishton, in "Anglican Schism," mentions no vestments as retained, but only cope and surplice 170, 171

Appendix III.

Rev. T. T. Carter's letter. Court of Final Appeal, judges, not whether documents true, but whether accredited teacher has, or has not, broken terms of understood contract 172-176

Appendix IV.

In solemn service, directed by Elizabeth, four months from enactment of Rubric, copes, not vestments, worn at Celebration 177-179

EDITIONS REFERRED TO.

AMES AND HERBERT, Typographical Antiquities, enlarged by T. F. Dibdin. London, 1810-19.

AUGUSTINI (S.), Opera Studio Monach: Ord. S. Benedicti. Parisiis, 1836-38.

Baxterianæ Reliquiæ, Sylvester. London, 1696.

BURNET, History of the Reformation. London, 1850.

———, History of his own Time. London, 1724-34.

CARDWELL, Conferences connected with the Revision of the Book of Common Prayer. Oxford, 1840.

——————— Documentary Annals of the Reformed Church of England. Oxford, 1839.

——————— Synodalia. Oxford, 1842.

Common Prayer, Facsimile of the Black Letter Book of 1836, containing the MS. alterations made in 1661. London, 1871.

CLARENDON, EDWARD, EARL OF, Life, by himself. Oxford, 1827.

COSIN's Works. Oxford, 1851.

——— Correspondence. Surtees Society. Part I. Durham, 1869; part II. Durham, 1872.

FLEURY, Histoire Ecclesiastique. Paris, 1725.

GARUCCI (RAFFAELE), D.C.D.G., Vetr. Ornati di figure in oro trovati nei cimiteri dei Cristiani primitivi di Roma. Roma, 1858.

GIBSON, Synodus Anglicana. By E. Gibson, D.D., afterwards Bishop of London; edited by E. Cardwell. Oxford, 1854.

GRINDAL, EDMUND, successively Bishop of London and Archbishop of York and Canterbury, Remains of. Parker Society. Cambridge, 1843.

HEYLYN, Ecclesia Restaurata, or History of the Reformation. Cambridge, 1849.

HIERONYMI, Opus Epistolarum divi Hieronymi Stridonensis, una cum Scholiis Des. Erasmi, denuo per illum recognitum. Apud Basileam, 1523.

Hierurgia Anglicana, edited by members of the Cambridge Camden Society. v. d.

Injunctions, geuen by the Queenes Majesty, Anno Domini 1559. The first yeere of the raigne of our Soveraigne Lady Queene Elizabeth. Cum privilegio Regiæ majestatis. With Jugge's title page border.

Editions referred to.

JOHNSON'S Dictionary, by Todd. London, 1818.
MALMESBIRIENSIS, Wilhelmi Monachi. Gesta Regum Anglorum et Historia Novella. Recensuit T. Duffus Hardy. London, 1840.
MARRIOTT, Rev. Wharton, B., M.A., F.S.A., Vestiarium Christianum. The Origin and Gradual Development of the Dress of Holy Ministry in the Church. London, 1868.
NICHOLS, JOHN, F.S.A., The Progresses and Public Processions of Queen Elizabeth; among which are interspersed other Solemnities, etc. Printed from original MSS., etc. London, 1788.
PARKER (Archbishop), Correspondence. Parker Society. Cambridge, 1853.
————, Mr. JAMES, Introduction to the Successive Revisions of the Book of Common Prayer. Oxford, 1877.
————, ————, Did Queen Elizabeth take other Order in the Advertisements of 1566? A Letter to Lord Selborne. Oxford, 1878.
————, Mr. J. H., Archaeology of Rome; Catacombs. London, 1877.
————, Mediaeval Church and Altar Decorations in Rome, and Mosaic Pictures in chronological order. London, 1876.
PEACOCK, English Church Furniture, Ornaments, etc. London, 1866.
RAINE, REV. JAMES, Vestments: what has been said and done about them in the Northern province since the Reformation. London and York, 1866.
Report (Second) of Commissioners appointed to inquire into the Rubrics, Orders, and Directions for Regulating the Course and Conduct of Public Worship. London, 1868.
ROCK, D., Hierurgia, or Transubstantiation, Invocation of Saints, Relics and Purgatory, besides those other Articles of Doctrine set forth in the Holy Sacrifice of the Mass. By D. Rock, D.D. 1851.
DE ROSSI, Cav. G. B., La Roma Sotterranea Cristiana, descritta ed Illustrata. Publicata per ordine della Santita de N.S. Papa Pio Nono. Roma, 1864-77.
SANDER, Rise and Growth of the Anglican Schism. By Nicholas Sander, D.D., sometime Fellow of New College, Oxford. Published A.D. 1585, with a continuation of the history, by Rev. Edward Rishton, B.A., of Brasenose, Oxford. Translated, with Introduction and Notes by David Lewis, M.A. London, 1877.
SELBORNE, Lord, Notes on some Passages in the Liturgical History of the Reformed English Church. London, 1878.
SPARROW, Collection of Articles, Injunctions, chiefly in the times of King Edward VI., Queen Elizabeth, King James, and King Charles I. Published to vindicate the Church of England, and to promote Peace in the same. London, 1634.
STRYPE, Annals of the Reformation. Oxford, 1824.

Editions referred to.

STRYPE, Life of Parker. Oxford, 1821.
———, ——— Grindal. Oxford, 1821.
———, ——— Aylmer. Oxford, 1821.
Surtees Society. Acts of High Commission Court, within the Diocese of Durham. Durham, 1858.
Statutes, Ecclesiastical and Eleemosynary. By A. J. Stephens. London, 1845.
WAKE, The State of the Church and Clergy. London, 1703.
WHITGIFT, JOHN, D.D., An Answere to a certen Libel, intituled An Admonition to the Parliament. London, 1572.
WILKINS, DAVID, S.T.P., Concilia Magnae Britanniae et Hiberniae, a Synodo Verolamiensi, A.D. 440, ad Londinensem, A.D. 1717. London, 1727.
Zurich Letters, comprising the correspondence of several English Bishops and others with some of the Helvetian Reformers during the early part of the reign of Queen Elizabeth. Parker Society. Cambridge, 1842.

THE CHURCH AND THE ORNAMENTS RUBRIC.

E. B. WHEATLEY BALME *to* REV. H. M. FLETCHER.

MY DEAR MR. FLETCHER,

I have to thank you for sending me the Address delivered by the President of the English Church Union, June 22, 1881.

I have carefully read Mr. Wood's paper. As you suggest an expression of opinion from me, I write on one point only in the vast subject, which, at present, presses strongly on my mind.

Since the time of the Gorham Judgment, I have been intensely anxious about encroachment by the State on the spiritual jurisdiction of the Church, to which I attach paramount importance. But, with regard to the aspect of the question now so prominent, I must say that the position taken up by the English Church Union for the battle of the Church against the State, seems to me strangely ill-chosen and illogical, viz. that on the Ornaments Rubric.

Mr. J. Parker, by his "Letter to Lord Selborne" and his "Introduction to the Revisions of the Book of Common Prayer," and my own examination of the contemporary documents to which he refers, have fully convinced me that the Ornaments Rubric was *an attempt* at legislation, *circa sacra*, by authority purely secular, steadfastly resisted by the Church. In it, Queen Elizabeth, Tudor like, tried to impose on the Church her own personal taste in matters of ritual. Her subservient Parliament obeyed her behest, and passed the Statute of Uniformity, from which the Ornaments Rubric was a modification of one clause. But every Bishop who was present in the House of Lords voted against the Bill. That was the only opportunity which the authorities of the Church had of giving official judgment upon it. The Queen took care that the Prayer-Book in which she had the rubric inserted, was never submitted to Convocation. But the mind of the Church was unmistakably expressed in act, or rather in passive resistance. So far as evidence has been produced, *not one parish priest ever conformed to it then, or for three hundred years afterwards.* If any evidence had been forthcoming, no doubt Mr. Parker, with his views and his research, would have produced it; but, on the contrary, he says[1] that the chasuble is never even mentioned in the contemporary documents. Yet many churches, at that time, had the vestments; as is proved by the returns as to their destruction, a few years later, in Lincoln Diocese and elsewhere. This fact disproves the theory which tries to account for their disuse on the ground of expense. The clergy had them, but *did not*

---

[1] "Letter to Lord Selborne," p. 96.

wear them. Yet many of these must have worn them in Queen Mary's time. Those who still kept to the Latin Mass—which the Queen kept for a time in her own chapel—no doubt continued to wear them; but of their use by a parish priest with the English Book in which the rubric was, there is not a trace that I have heard of. Under these circumstances, the disuse amounts to positive rejection. The Queen, strong in head and will, as she was, found the resistance of the Church too strong for her, and she never even attempted to enforce her rubric as to the "ornaments of the ministers." She did try hard to enforce the crucifix as one of the ornaments of the Church, threatening the Bishops with deprivation unless they consented. But they stood firm, and she was foiled, so completely, at last, that the crucifix in her own chapel was, *horribile dictu*, broken by the Court fool, and never replaced.[1] During her own long reign, nobody ventured to alter her rubric; and, after that, it had become so utterly a dead letter that nobody cared to alter it. It was simply ignored. The Convocation of Canterbury, in 1604, and of York, in 1605, dealing formally and synodically with the same matter, entirely ignored the rubric, and recognized *only the Advertisements.* The Canterbury Convocation of 1661, retained the rubric, with only verbal alteration conforming it to the statute, instead of to the Prayer-Book, of Elizabeth. In this they simply maintained the *status quo*, when the modified sense—in which only the rubric was ever practically accepted by the Church—had been fully established, by its coexistence with general non-user of the vestments, for an entire century.

[1] Heylyn, "Hist. Reform.," Elizabeth, Ann. 2.

The theory now set up is, that by this retention they intended to revive the use of the vestments so long disused. But all the ingenuity lavished in special pleading for it, fails to reconcile this theory with the broad fact, that not one priest of the Lower House of that Convocation, has been shown ever to have used them; nor one Bishop of the Upper, to have suggested that his clergy should use them, even by a question in Visitation Articles as to whether they did so. Yet never, during three centuries, was there an opportunity so favourable for the introduction of such ritual, as then, when they were on the crest of the wave of reaction against Puritanism.

It may be argued with much more force, that they intended to sanction the practice of moving the altar, at the time of celebration, and placing it tablewise " in the body of the church," or in the part of " the chancel where Morning, etc., Prayers be appointed to be said;" because they retained the rubric to that effect. Yet this was done with great deliberation. The MS. of their alterations shows that they first struck out the old rubric, and substituted one directing that " the table shall stand in the most convenient place in the upper end of ye chancell (or of ye body of ye church where there is no chancel)," but that, on final revision, they again struck out their new rubric and reinstated the old one. It may be argued that they, by this, deliberately sanctioned the " tablewise "—and rejected the " altarwise "—position. This argument is much stronger than that for the revival of the vestments; not only because of the final rejection of a change once adopted, but because the tablewise position was in frequent use both before and after 1661, but the vestments in neither period. It seems to me clear that, in their retention of both rubrics, the Revisers were actuated by the policy which has so often prevailed, of *quieta non movere*. Maintenance of the *status quo*, seemed the safest way to avoid stirring the embers of questions, which had been previously, and might again become (as we painfully feel one of them now) fiercely burning questions. In both cases the Revisers' own practice contravened the letter of the rubrics which they retained; and in both cases the general practice of the Church, has done the same. It rejected the "tablewise" position of the altar on the whole, though not without considerable diversity. It rejected the vestments with unanimity unparalleled, and unbroken for three whole centuries.

How the "living voice of the Church" could have pronounced on a rule of practice for the clergy, more distinctly than by the *consensus* in actual practice, of the whole *clerus*, for so long a period, I cannot conceive.

The English Church Union, then, in taking its stand upon Elizabeth's rubric, in her sense of it, while professing (no doubt with the utmost sincerity) to stand up for Church-made law against State-made law, is, in fact, doing just the opposite. It is setting up a rule of discipline which a Queen tried to impose upon the Church by parliamentary sanction only—*against* that which "this Church hath received" by the consentient practice of the whole *clerus* (whom it specially concerns), as of one man, for three centuries.

The rubric bears, on the face of it, the stamp of "Cæsar's image and superscription." It bases its command solely on "the authority of Parliament." "It was itself copied from a clause in an Act of Parliament. Its legal interpretation is a question of the interpretation of three Acts of Parliament. Of such interpretation, I think it must be admitted that secular lawyers are the most competent judges. Τά Καίσαρος Καίσαρι. On this point, too, the position taken by the English Church Union seems utterly untenable. It appeals to Cæsar's law, while denying Cæsar's jurisdiction to interpret that law.

Yours very sincerely,

E. B. WHEATLEY BALME.

Rev. H. M. Fletcher *to* E. B. Wheatley Balme.

Dear Mr. Wheatley Balme,

You say that the position taken up by the English Church Union for the battle of the Church against the State seems to you strangely ill-chosen and illogical, viz. that on the Ornaments Rubric. But I would ask—Has the English Church Union *chosen* it? Men must defend where they are attacked, and the attacked clergy have been attacked and condemned, principally, on the ground of using certain ornaments, which they use, being, as they believe, justified, if not obliged, in the matter, by the Ornaments Rubric. Would you have had the English Church Union stand still and see them attacked and condemned without doing aught in their defence? On which ever side justice lay the case would have gone by default against the attacked, if his case had not been pleaded. You will say, "The attacked has in most cases refused to plead, denying the jurisdiction of the Court." The Commission now sitting shows that there may be good grounds for the denying it. If the English Church Union had sought to *force* on any clergyman the observance of laws long with impunity broken, and had chosen from among the many rubrics thus broken the Ornaments Rubric for the battlefield, then I should have agreed with you, that it had taken up a position very *ill-chosen*, if I could not have quite seen with you that it was illogical.

Queen Elizabeth's Ornaments Rubric, you are convinced, was an attempt at legislation, *circa sacra*, by authority purely secular. I am not concerned to deny this. But this is not the rubric which is our law; and our law, the rubric of 1662, is a piece of legislation, *circa sacra*, coming to us with *all possible authority*—a law, first, of the Church, speaking through its Convocations, its voice endorsed by the sovereign; then, secondly, of the State acting constitutionally: The sovereign, "by and with the advice of his Parliament," enacted what *was* Church law into statute law. Whatever vice there was in the original promulgation of Elizabeth's Rubric, erecting, by parliamentary authority alone, a standard for the Church, has been completely avoided in the case of the Rubric which has been the constitutional law (of both Church and State) since 1662. However, between 1559 and 1662, Queen Elizabeth's Rubric may have been resisted by the Church, the existing Rubric was by the Church herself set up as *her* standard in 1662. *All reference to Elizabeth's statute* was removed from it, and *that standard* was fixed for the Church's law which had existed in Edward VI.'s second year by authority of Parliament. A Parliament of Churchmen had, before a certain year (2nd Edward VI.), stamped with its authority, and made English law, the use of certain vestments, always hitherto in use in the Church of England, and had commanded *their* continued use. The Church and Parliament of 1662 knew that various changes in the law and practice of the Church of England had been made in the hundred and thirteen years which had elapsed, culminating in the overthrow of crown and altar; and having, on the restoration of these, to choose *what* standard it would now raise, deliberately chose, instead of the standard of James, or of Elizabeth, or of Mary, or of the later years of Edward VI., that of his second *year*. The Church had seen her laws violated, her practice lowered, and her doctrine degraded, and God had shown her the end of such courses; and she, as it seems to me, most wisely, raised the standard to its old height, and bade her children aim at it, while, like a tender mother, she refrained from forcing them up to it. It is a mark of the slowness of her children to learn wisdom that it has taken two hundred years to bring many of them up to it. When doctrine is apprehended, obedience to the Church's rules follows, and it is seen how truly her ritual is the proper shrine for her doctrine. In the Tudor days the Church, as represented by Bishops and Convocation, often changed its mind; but the truth never changed.

You say, " every Bishop present in the House voted against Elizabeth's Bill." I suppose they were in great part nominees of Edward VI. and his foreign Protestant advisers. They probably disobeyed the law? Then they were like Mr. Green. But not even Queen Elizabeth imprisoned them for contempt. Hanoverian rule is harder here than Tudor. Did Convocation protest against her Bill? or did she terrify it into submission? Anyhow, you are convinced, by lack of evidence to the contrary, that every parish priest in England disobeyed the law, and you think they were justified in doing so. If we all, then, agreed to disobey the Public Worship Regulation Act, should we be justified? I say, *Yes, in foro conscientiæ*, but that we ought not to "grumble at the consequences." But is it wise of a State to pass laws which thus aggrieve the consciences of some of her best subjects? To this there can be but one answer, I think. From 1559 onwards the Bishops seem to have been as disobedient as the priests. There is no provision for them in the advertisements.

You write from memory as to Parker's Letter, saying that there is no mention in contemporary documents of "chasubles." But if these documents abound with mention of "vestments," and if that word "vestment" *then* was the common word, as I believe it was, for the particular vestment "the chasuble," then the *thing* is there, though not the *name*.

I know not whose the *theory* is that they were *disused* on account of the expense. Their *non-use, after their destruction*, is easily explained on the score of expense in again supplying them. No doubt many of the Puritan clergy had them and did not use them; but have you historical memorials enough of the practice of country parishes—the most conservative places—to entitle you to say that the clergy generally did not use them? There must have been hundreds of clergy who lived through the reigns of Edward VI., and Mary, and into Elizabeth's who were old Catholics at heart, and who would naturally cling to the use of all that was legal, and, till evidence from a great part of the country is forthcoming that the old vestments were not worn, I shall continue to hold it most probable that in very many old parishes the old vestments *were* worn. Is there any extant proof of a Bishop reproving any priest or bringing him into court for wearing a chasuble?

You say, "The Queen . . . never even attempted to enforce the rubric as to the Ornaments Rubric." I grant you she did not to the full extent of it. That she desired to enforce some parts of it is proved by her order to the Archbishop to issue advertisements, and *his* advertisements prove how far *he* was disposed to go on the road she wished pursued, as *her* displeasure with *his* advertisements, and her refusal through Cecil to endorse them, shows how much further she wished to go in the way of enforcing. That her not enforcing the rubric after the issue of the advertisements is not a good argument against the contention that the rubric was still law, is shown by the consideration that neither Queen nor Bishop has sought to enforce the Ridsdale Judgment, which yet is in their eyes "law." A wise authority may very well dispense with enforcing a law when it perceives that the subject is at the time "unable to bear it," and yet may refuse to alter the standard of law when convinced that it is the *right* one. The advertisements were disobeyed as well as the law of the rubric, and yet, according to the view (I suppose from what you write) of the Convocations of 1603 and 1605, *they* were law of the Church as well as of the realm "rejected by the very Bishops who issued them." But in what sense did *these* Convocations read the advertisements? Surely as prescribing a minimum, not as overriding the rubric or altering the standard there set up. If they had wished to do this, how easy *then* to have stated what standard they wished adopted, for they would have found no difficulty with the Parliament of the day.

I must entreat you to reconsider the statement, that the

Convocations *retained* the rubric with only verbal alterations, etc. They were legislating after sixteen years of "no Prayer-Book" and "no rubric." They *reverted*, if you will, to a Prayer-Book which it had been declared a crime to use, and in that Prayer-Book they found a rubric setting up a standard of ornaments of Church and minister, and they resolved to re-erect the same standard. But whereas the old rubric as it stood in 1603 concluded with "according to the Act of Parliament set in the beginning of this book," they erased these words, for what other conceivable purpose than to show that they sought no other authority for their standard than that which was inherent in themselves? They acted in the spirit of the closing paragraph of the thirty-fourth Article. They were free to adopt a standard which in a certain year had been sealed with the authority of Parliament, and they did adopt it, but that Act of Parliament in Edward VI.'s time was not their authority in 1662 for acting. It was their own choice in the exercise of their own authority, and again Parliament sealed the Church's choice of a standard. They did not—excuse me for saying it—maintain the *status quo*, not even the *status quo ante bellum*.

By this "retention" you say, rather I would say by this "reintroduction" of the old standard—seldom or never reached, I will allow—but still bearing witness as it stood to the mind of the Reformers, or of the mind of the Queen when the Reformers had been impregnated with foreign heresies, and when the Queen, hard as she was, was the truer representative of the English Catholic Church, they declared their mind.

The English Church Union, in defending the attacked, takes

its stand, not on Elizabeth's rubric, in her sense of it, but on the rubric of the Sealed Book in its grammatical sense, as expounded by the highest law officers of the Crown, and so must be allowed to stand up for Church-made law and State-made law, against a wrongful statement of the conditions of the law.

Our rubric does not base its command solely on the authority of Parliament. The authority of Parliament *is necessary* to give coercive force in the courts of the sovereign to the laws of the Church, and it is therefore well always, in a Prayer-Book intended to be coercive, to cite it; but in the Ornaments Rubric its authority is mentioned in connection with a date, much as the words "under Pontius Pilate" are recited in the Creed.

Lastly, have Bishops and great officers of other degrees in the Church paid more attention to the "canons and constitutions of the Church" since 1605 than they have done to State-made law, granting for a moment that what the English Church Union defends *is* State-made law; and if they have not, is it endurable that they should sanction prosecutions of the inferior clergy for breach of the decisions of the Judicial Committee of Council? Does *their* non-user of the cope amount to *rejection* by the Church of her own law? and if it does not, why should the non-user of the chasuble by the parochial clergy amount to rejection on the part of the Church of the *State-made law*, if we grant that it is State-made law?

Is not the truth, after all, this, that the state of the Church of England has been one in many respects like that of the Jewish Church between Solomon and Josiah—utter disregard of its high ideal, till the attempt to realize it seems to many a revolution instead of a reformation. It is a mere accident that the fight is about *vestments*. They would never have been attacked, but that the old Catholic doctrine of the primitive Church is, in the eyes of those who attack them, a heresy, and men must see whether it is so or not. God's providence it is, rather than an accident, and He will make the truth prevail.

Yours always most sincerely,
HENRY M. FLETCHER.

November 18, 1881.

SECOND LETTER *from* E. B. WHEATLEY BALME *to* REV. H. M. FLETCHER.

MY DEAR MR. FLETCHER.

Will you allow me to answer some of the questions put or raised in your letter?

You ask, "'Have you historical memorials enough of the practice of country parishes—the most conservative places—to entitle you to say that the clergy generally did not use" the vestments?

The question is perfectly fair and pertinent. It is, no doubt, difficult to prove a negative in the face of wide possibilities.

But I submit in this case, that the *onus probandi*, that the clergy *did* use the vestments, lies on those who affirm that such use is part of "the discipline which this Church has received." Under this protest, I submit further, that there is such a "conspicuous absence" of positive evidence for the use, where one might reasonably expect to find it, as strongly points to a negative conclusion.

§ I.—ABSENCE OF EVIDENCE FOR USE OF THE VESTMENTS.

I. I refer again to Mr. James Parker. His historical researches have eminently qualified him for the inquiry. His

"Introduction to the Revisions of the Book of Common Prayer" is a storehouse of information relating to the subject. He is a zealous advocate of the parliamentary authority of the vestments. But, so far from producing evidence that they were ever used under Elizabeth's rubric, he says,[1] speaking of the "evidence whether of official or unofficial documents," that there is "mention only of the surplice and cope both before 1566 and after, as being the only vestments for the Holy Communion, and that albe and chasuble had gone out of use." If they were not used before 1566 under authority of the rubric, when were they used?

II. I received lately, by post, a paper marked "Important." It is a reprint by the English Church Union from the *Spectator*, of a review of a recent book, "Chronicles of the Collegiate Church or Free Chapel of All Saints', Derby." The reviewer begins by saying that he "calls attention" to the volume because "it casts an important light on the Ritualistic controversy." He then goes into the familiar arguments against the legal authority of the Advertisements; "speaks of thousands of clergy who performed divine service according to the ritual of the first Prayer-Book of Edward VI.," after the Advertisements; and "concludes with the evidence furnished by the inventories in the church of All Saints', Derby," in the "words of the editors of the volume," who say "it will be noted that the vestments were used at All Saints' for more than a decade after the alleged Advertisements of Privy Council fame."

Having been long in search of such evidence, I somewhat

[1] "Letter to Lord Selborne," p. 98.

rashly ordered the book. It is a highly "got up," and, as my bookseller's bill proves, a costly *edition de luxe*. I find the statement of the editors, who base it on the fact that copes are mentioned in the inventories till the 10th of Elizabeth (1567-8), but albs are enumerated, year by year, up to the 19th of Elizabeth (1576-7). Upon this I must observe—

1. That the mention of church goods in an inventory is no proof that they were *used*. Future editors of chronicles of Durham, might infer from inventories, that copes have been used there, all the present century; but we have recently seen the Dean of Durham making public confession of his own, and his predecessor's, shortcomings in that respect.

2. That the *use* of *copes* in a *collegiate* church would be in strict accordance with the practice which was, no doubt, received by the Reformed Church, and embodied in the Advertisements, and the Canons of 1604; and which, though often neglected, has always been more or less recognized. But this proves nothing as to the observance of Elizabeth's Rubric.

3. That the mention of albs proves as little.

I understand that the word vestment is sometimes taken to include the accessories, alb, etc.; but I never heard that "alb" could include "vestment."

4. But in an inventory of 1560-1, on the previous page of the Chronicles, appears "a fyne vestment that Mr. Royd gave." This was presumably a new vestment given late in the time of Queen Mary—who "appointed two vicars to serve at All Saints' "--or very early in the reign of Elizabeth. If so, it

c

could hardly have been worn out in three years. But from the inventory of 1563-4 this vestment *disappears*, and only copes and an "aube" remain. Whatever might be the cause, Mr. Royd's "fyne vestment" was no longer there. It might be there without being used; but it could hardly be used when it was not there. Therefore, this "important evidence" adduced by the English Church Union to prove the use of the vestments— while it does not prove at all that they were *used* under Elizabeth's Rubric—does prove that, in a church where the vicars appointed by Queen Mary, were peculiarly likely to have retained, and used their accustomed vestments, within four years from the issue of the rubric, a chasuble was no longer even found.

III. I have searched, as well as I could, Strype's voluminous and disjointed collections of the period, for evidence of the use of the vestments; but have found none where one would expect to find it, if the use existed; *e.g.* he prints[1] a paper among the Secretary's MSS., dated February, 1564-5, apparently intended as an exhaustive list of the varieties then existing in parish churches, as to divine service and the administration of the Sacraments. It gives full and minute particulars under each head, but it makes no mention of the vestments. Within five years, then, from the issue of Elizabeth's Rubric, the use of the vestments was non-existent, or so rare as to be unknown to one so conversant with the ecclesiastical affairs of the period, *quarum pars magna fuit*, as Secretary Cecil; who probably had before him the returns required by the

[1] Strype, Archbishop Parker, i. 302.

Queen's letter of the previous month as to "diversities in ceremonies and rites" (see *infra*, p. 41).

IV. Cosin, in his Third Series of notes on the Prayer-Book, says,[1] "It was well known that Lord Treasurer Burleigh used them" (altar lights previously mentioned) "constantly in his chapel, with other ornaments of fronts, palls, and books upon his altar." But he does *not* mention with these ornaments, the use of vestments. The omission is very significant, especially when we observe the changes in Cosin's treatment of the question. In the First Series he claims for the use of the vestments, the authority of Convocation.[2] "If," he says, "that authority be the Convocation of the clergy, as I think it is (only that), the fourteenth canon commands us to observe all the ceremonies prescribed in this book." But then, with reference to the objection that "now the fifty-eighth canon hath appointed it otherwise," he adds, "I would fain know how we should observe both canons." The ingenious solution of the difficulty, which he states and leaves unsolved, by the modern theory of a *maximum* and *minimum*, was undreamt of by him. Indeed, the terms of the fourteenth canon, which he was quoting, are wholly incompatible with that theory; for it commands the ceremonies of the Prayer-Book to be observed "without any addition or diminution." But a *minimum* necessarily implies diminution from a *maximum*.

When the case of the Durham vestments came in question, Cosin seems to have arrived at a different opinion. Whether he had come to think that the specific directions of the fifty-eighth

[1] Works, v. 441.   [2] Ibid. v. 43.

canon at least, were not superseded by the general directions of the fourteenth; or that the vestments were not within the purview of the latter canon; or for whatever reason, he then admitted, both in word and deed, that the vestments did not come to be "according to the canons and constitutions of the Church,"[1] till they were altered and changed into copes. Accordingly, in his Second and Third Series of notes, he no longer appeals to the law of the Church for them, or for the "ornaments of the church;" but to the law of the realm, *viz.* "to the authority of Parliament," a phrase which he reiterates again and again. Mr. Parker observes,[2] "The attention, and one may say deference, to Acts of Parliament shown by Cosin throughout his Notes is remarkable." Cosin was arming himself for conflict with his puritanical adversary, Peter Smart. That very unamiable clergyman—whose conscientiousness, however, according to his lights, I see no reason to doubt—certainly got the worst of it. His case went far beyond Mr. Green's. He was,[3] August 3, 1630, "ordered to make recantation, *conceptis verbis*, at three several places in York and Durham; to be suspended totally *ab officio*; fined £400; to pay costs of suit; committed to prison, September 2nd; excommunicated for not performing his submission, November 10th; all his ecclesiastical livings sequestered November 18th; degraded ab omni gradu et dignitate clericali, because he did not recant and pay costs; kept in prison till 1641,"[4] when the general temporary triumph of puritanism turned the tables for the short remainder of his life.

[1] *Infra*, p. 88.   [2] Introduction, p. 343.
[3] Surtees Society. Court of High Commission, at Durham. App. p. 206.
[4] Ibid., p. 240.

The English Church Union is engaged in a similar conflict now. But it differs from Cosin, in that he did not, while basing his argument for vestments and ornaments on the "authority of Parliament," claim that such questions should be determined exclusively by the authority of the Church. He did not deny the competency of judges appointed by the State to interpret laws passed by the State; to interpret, on behalf of the State, the terms of the implied compact by which the clergy hold property and privilege. He did not, at the same time, appeal to Cæsar, and repudiate Cæsar's jurisdiction. This is what the English Church Union is now doing. This inconsistency I venture to call illogical. While writing the above, I laid down my pen and took up the *Literary Churchman* of December 9, 1881, and there found (p. 525) the real point at issue [1] disentangled from the mass of confusion in which it has been involved, and stated with admirable clearness by Mr. T. T. Carter; a name which must carry great weight with all those who generally agree with him, as it is justly venerated by many who on some points differ from him.

But to return from this digression, and from Cosin as a litigant, to Cosin as a witness touching the use of the vestments. It would have been much to his purpose if the information which enabled him to speak of it as "well known," that the ornaments of the church which he mentions, were used in Lord Burleigh's Chapel, had extended to the use of the vestments there. That Cosin omits any mention of these, is strong evidence that they were not known to have been used in the

[1] See Appendix III.

place where, next to the Queen's own chapel, we should most have expected to find the use. Burleigh, from his own taste, or in deference to that of his royal mistress, or both, was inclined to elaborate ritual. When Guest, on behalf of the divines selected by Cecil[1] to revise the Prayer-Book, had sent it to him with the direction for the use of the surplice only, as in 1552; he suggested "whether, in the celebration of the Holy Communion, priests should not use a cope besides a surplice." Though Guest,[2] on behalf of the revising divines, still maintained the sufficiency of the surplice, the Act of Uniformity was passed with the proviso for retaining the ornaments of 1549. Cecil, from his position, must have had a leading part in this legislation; as Sandys, who was another Reviser, in the same letter[3] in which he informs Parker of what had been done in Parliament, adds, "Mr. Secretary is earnest with the book." It is highly probable that the Rubric, following the Act, was inserted by him under the Queen's command. If so, it becomes still more remarkable that the vestments were not known to have been used in his chapel, as well as the other ornaments which were known; yet the fact agrees with what we find elsewhere, that in the Queen's own chapel it was the cope that was used rather than the vestments.[4]

V. In the Convocation of 1562, thirty-two of the puritanically disposed members of the Lower House—headed by Nowel,

[1] Strype, Annals, vol. i. pt. i. 120.
[2] Appendix, Strype's Annals, vol. i. pt. ii. Book III. No. 14.
[3] Burnet, Reformation: Records, vol. ii. pt. iii. No. 2. Parker Correspondence, p. 65.
[4] See Heylyn, Reformation Ann. Eliz. 2. See *infra*, Appendix II. and IV.

Dean of St. Paul's, and Sampson of Christ Church, afterwards deprived for nonconformity [1]—put in seven articles, requesting that "playing of organs may be removed;" that they may leave off the sign of the cross in baptism, as a thing "of which many have conceived superstitious opinions;" that "in the time of ministering the Communion, kneeling may be left indifferent;" that the *use of copes and surplices* may be taken away," etc. Now, is it conceivable that men bent on making so clean a sweep of what they deemed superstitious, would, while condemning the use of copes and surplices, have left unchallenged the use of the special vestments of the Mass, if they had known such use to exist? or that the use could have existed unknown to six Deans, twelve Archdeacons, and fourteen Proctors of the clergy, or any of them? If not, where were the "thousands of clergy throughout the land," whom the imagination of the English Church Union reviewer of Chronicles of All Saints' Derby, pictures "performing service according to the ritual of the first Prayer-Book of Edward VI.;" or even the "hundreds" you "think" there must have been? I have hitherto failed to find positive evidence of the period, for *one*.

VI. I have carefully searched the two big octavos of what Mr. Parker may well call the "great Zürich series" of letters. Here are nearly three hundred documents, beginning with 1559, the year in which the Ornaments Rubric appeared, and extending, more or less, over the next twenty years. Many of them are a kind of news-letters whereby Bishops, clergy, and others in England, give to their friends at Zürich, full details as to

---

[1] Strype, Annals, vol. i. pt. i. p. 500.

Church matters in the former country. They are especially full on the vestiarian question, then, as now, fiercely burning. Some of the English writers were intensely puritanical; others moderate Reformers. Gualter, writing in 1572,[1] says of himself and Bullinger—who were the two at Zurich most frequently addressed—that "letters on both sides were sent to them almost every day, while that unhappy controversy about the habits was agitated." Those of the puritanical party, are full of fierce invective about the "dregs of popery" still retained in the English Church, especially the dress used in divine service. Now, I must again urge that if the clergy had been, to any appreciable extent, using, under the English Service Book, the same vestments which had been so long—and up to a period then so recent—associated with the Latin Mass, it is to me absolutely inconceivable that men, in the state of mind in which these puritanical writers were, could have forborne from seizing and dwelling upon a topic so directly apposite to their purpose. That would have been as if, in files of the *Rock* or the *Record* for the last twenty years, no mention were to be found of "ritualistic practices." But wherever in these letters the "popish vestments" are specified as in actual use, it is clear that the surplice and cope, not the alb and chasuble, are meant. To take one or two instances out of many. Sampson, Dean of Christ Church—who was the leader of the thirty-seven suspended, and was himself ultimately deprived for refusing to conform and subscribe to the advertisements—with Humphrey, and others like minded, carry on a lengthened correspondence

[1] Zürich Letters, p. 363.

with Bullinger and Gualter, in order to enlist the latter on their side in the battle which they claim to be fighting against the relics of popery still retained in the English Church. With that view they bring up all the evidence they can to prove the existence of such relics; *e.g.* they append to a letter of July, 1566,[1] a formal list of thirteen "maculæ quæ in ecclesiâ Anglicanâ adhuc hærent. . . . 5. In coenâ Dominicâ sacræ vestes, nempe *copa* et *superpelliceum* adhibentur."

Neither here, nor in the many other places where they speak of the *habitus papisticus*, is there anything that can be understood to refer to the chasuble and alb. The only passage in which I have been able to find any possible reference to these is in Bullinger's letter of May 1, 1566, to which they were replying.[2] "Nunquam probaverim, si vestrum jubeamini exequi ministerium, ad aram crucifixi imagine oneratam magis quam ornatam, et in veste missaticâ, hoc est in albâ et in copâ quae a tergo quoque ostentet crucifixi imaginem. Attamen ex literis allatis ex Anglia intelligo, *nulla* nunc *est de ejusmodi vestitu contentio*, sed quaestio est an liceat ministris Evangelicis portare . . . vestem albam quam vocant superpelliceum."

Here it seems probable that Bullinger, not being much versed in *vestiarian* nomenclature, uses the word *copa* by mistake for *casula*. The association with the alb, and the image of the crucifix *a tergo*, were characteristic of the latter, which also was specially *vestis missatica*. On the other hand, the *copa was* ordered in England for cathedrals, etc., by the Advertise-

---

[1] Zürich Letters, Epist. lxxi. App. p. 97.
[2] Burnet, Reformation Records, pt. iii. Book VI. No. 73.

ments then recently issued. Of this, Sampson and Humphrey take care to inform Bullinger, both in the body of their letter replying to this, and in their appended list of *maculæ*;[1] but they do not dispute Bullinger's assertion that the *restitus* properly called *missatica*, was wholly *out of the question*. This omission on their part, when their attention was specially directed to the point, amounts to an admission that, though Bullinger might be mistaken as to the name of a garment, the information contained in his "almost daily" letters from England, was substantially correct.

Supposing that when he wrote *copa* he meant *casula*, this would form the only exception that I have been able to find to Mr. Parker's statement as to the period, "that while the evidence adduced, whether in official or unofficial documents, shows that the surplices and copes were understood to be ordered, rare mention is made of albs, and none of chasubles whatever."[2]

This is as to the *use* of the vestments under the Ornaments Rubric. They are mentioned in inventories as *existing* down to the time of the Advertisements, and, in a few cases, later.

But evidence against the *use* appears at a very early date. On April 1, 1560, nearly six years before the issue of the Advertisements, and scarcely one after that of the Ornaments Rubric, Sandys, then Bishop of Worcester, writing to Peter Martyr,[3] mentions the Queen's attempt to enforce the use of the crucifix; for resisting which, he says, "*non multum aberat quin et ab officio amoverer et principis indignationem incur-*

---

[1] See above, p. 25.   [2] Letter to Lord Selborne, p. 96.
[3] Zürich Letters, Epist. xxxi. App. p. 43.

rerem; and proceeds "At Deus, in cujus manu sunt corda regum . . . ecclesiam Anglicanam ab hujusmodi offendiculis liberavit. *Tantum* manent in ecclesia nostra vestimenta illa papistica (*copas intellige*) quas diu non duraturas speramus." Sandys, by his *copas intellige*, clearly implies that Martyr was not to understand, on the one hand, the surplice—which Sandys approved of, though Martyr might not—nor, on the other, the special vestments of the Latin Mass, which both would have deemed still more popish, and graver *offendicula* than the copes. Sandys could hardly have written thus if he had known the vestments to be then in use. Yet few men had better opportunities of knowing than he, as Bishop of a midland see; one of the Queen's commissioners for the ecclesiastical visitation of the north; and taking an active part in Church matters in the metropolis. On the whole, the conclusion irresistibly forced on my mind by these contemporary documents, is, that when the Latin Mass ceased to be used, the use of the vestments distinctively associated with it, ceased also. It seems to me certain, that from the time when Elizabeth's Rubric appeared in the English Service Book, making the proviso of the Act of Uniformity into a direct command, by changing the "retained and be in use" of the proviso, into the "ministers shall use" of the Rubric, the clergy, who only could act, presented an unbroken front of passive and silent resistance. They simply did it not, and said nothing about it. It is very remarkable how, at a time when the air was as full of controversy about vestments as it is now, this rubric, of which we now hear so much—though then newly ushered into the world under the auspices of a mighty Queen and her Parliament, led by a most able minister—is, in these documents treating on the same subject-matter, utterly ignored. What is most strange, the bitterest Puritans have not a word to say against it. On the other hand, the Bishops and others, who; under strong though variable pressure by the Queen, and from their own desire for peace; were most anxious to win over the objectors to the use of the surplice, are equally silent about the Rubric. On the theory that it continued in force as a *maximum*, it would have been most natural for the Bishops to point out to these "nonconformitans" that it was to a *minimum* only, that they were required to conform, instead of to a *maximum* much more distasteful to them, which might have been legally enforced. But no trace of such an argument appears. Bullinger's argument with them, founded on his frequent communications with both parties in England, treats the use of the mass vestments, not as a thing which might have been enforced upon them, but as a thing entirely out of the question.

§ II. THE ADVERTISEMENTS.

The theory that the Advertisements were intended to enforce a *minimum*, leaving the Rubric as a maximum, is wholly inconsistent with their very *raison d'être*, as set forth in the preface, which recites that [1] "The Queen's Majesty, calling to remembrance how necessary it is that the State ecclesiastical be

---

[1] Wilkin, Concilia, vol. iv. p. 247; Sparrow Collection, p. 122.

conjoined in one uniformity of rites and manners in open prayer and ministration of sacraments . . . hath, by her letters, directed unto the Archbishop of Canterbury and Metropolitan, enjoined that *some order be taken* whereby all *diversities* and *varieties* among them of the clergy and people . . . might be *reformed* and repressed, and brought to *one manner* of *uniformity throughout* the *whole realm.*"

A *maximum* and a *minimum* of ritual, necessarily imply diversity, and are the antipodes to uniformity. To sanction such a *maximum* and *minimum* would have been to establish diversity instead of "the one manner of uniformity throughout the whole realm," which it was the Queen's special object to enforce.

State legislation, *circa sacra*, generally aims at uniformity, on the ground given in this preface, viz. that "diversities and varieties among them of the clergy and people breed nothing but contentions," which civil government abhors. This has been notably the case in England since the Reformation. All the Acts relating to the Prayer-Book have been Acts *for* UNIFORMITY.

Personally, I think that this straining after an uniformity, which the variety of men's minds, constitutions, and tastes, renders practically unattainable, has been a great misfortune to the English Church. I greatly desiderate a large liberty in the matter of ritual. I abhor with all my heart the narrow-minded bigotry which has prompted the recent prosecutions, and which has exhibited its virulence by keeping a conscientious clergyman in prison for nineteen months. I hope and believe that the outcome of the present struggle will be wider allowance for diversity of circumstances and of tastes. But, as a matter of history, the modern theory, that a *maximum* and a *minimum* of ritual was intended under the ecclesiastical legislation of the Tudors and Stuarts, seems to me to be (except as to the obvious distinction between cathedral, etc., and ordinary parish churches) absolutely without foundation; and merely an ingenious device suggested by the exigencies of recent controversy.

As to the use of the mass vestments under Elizabeth's Act and Rubric, the comment with which Sandys in the letter before referred to (p. 22), accompanied his announcement to Parker, seems to have proved truly prophetic of what, in fact, took place. He writes:[1] "The Book of Service is gone through with a proviso to retain the ornaments which were in the church in the first and second years of King Edward VI., until it pleases the Queen to take other order for them. Our gloss upon this text, is, that we shall not be forced to use them, but that others in the meantime shall not convey them away, but that they may remain for the Queen."

So, in effect, it proved. The clergy were not forced, and did not choose, to use the vestments. The peculation of valuable church goods, which had been going on both in Edward VI. and Mary's time, rendered needful such a proviso that these should be " retained," so that " others in the meantime should not carry them away." Sandys' "in the meantime" marks the merely temporary character then ascribed to the proviso, which in the Act itself was as clearly expressed by

[1] Parker Correspondence, p. 65.

the word "until." Since then the question has frequently been argued as if, in place of "until," the word had been "unless," which would have given the enactment quite a different character. Sandys, by his "they shall remain for the Queen," euphemistically intimates the light in which this piece of legislation was regarded—as an ecclesiastical hobby of the Queen's.

Elizabeth, no doubt, tried to convert the temporary proviso of the Act into a permanent rule, by inserting the Rubric in the Service Book. But this piece of "public worship regulation" by secular authority, proved still-born, and as absolutely inoperative as the Ecclesiastical Titles' Act of our own times. Taught by her defeat by the Bishops as to the crucifix, she was, as Sandys anticipated, too well advised to enter into a conflict with the whole body of the clergy unanimously occupying the strongest of positions, viz. that of simply passive resistance.

Here, then, we may read an explanation of the otherwise almost inexplicable silence as to the Rubric before and during the controversy about vestments. Nobody seems to have even thought of conforming to it; but a mixture, perhaps, of politeness to a lady, with certainly a discreet regard to what might follow from the displeasure of one so strong-minded and strong-handed, suggested the policy of "we never mention it" as safest. We may imagine how galling the sense of such a *fiasco* must have been to a Tudor sovereign, trained in the traditions of her race to regard the direction of matters ecclesiastical as a special function of her personal government. The soreness may be traced, five or six years later, in her capricious conduct as to the issue of the Advertisements. But, for the time, silent inaction was probably, under the circumstances, on her part the most dignified, as on that of her subjects the safest course to pursue. A formal repeal of her own special piece of Church legislation, would have been a confession of defeat too patent and humiliating for such a spirit to brook; and, practically, no repeal was needed of a law absolutely inoperative. So, the Rubric remained enthroned in the Prayer-Book; and soon proved itself a King Log so harmless that nobody (except Puritans trying to get rid of the surplice[1]) cared to disturb its peaceful *fainéant* reign of three centuries, till modern controversy—seizing on an *obiter dictum* of the judges in Liddell *v.* Westerton, when the question of the ornaments of ministers was not before them—metamorphosed it into the redoubtable King Stork we now behold, with the English Church Union for his bodyguard, and its President as commander-in-chief of the English clergy, with a special provost-marshalship over the Bishops.

The "Zürich Letters" prove the silence of the puritanical party; and explain the absence on their part of any complaint against the Rubric. They were quiet and contented because their goods were in peace. "Much of the law being," as Mr. Parker observes,[2] "a dead letter," they did as they pleased. Humphrey and Sampson wrote in 1566, *libertate in qua hactenus stetimus.*[3]

---

[1] Letter to Lord Selborne, p. 26.
[2] Zürich Letters, App. Epist. lxxi. p. 95.
[3] See *infra*, p. 137.

But before the beginning of the previous year, the Queen had been roused from her Achillean inaction by sundry reports which she had heard,[1] that "there was crept and brought into the Church by some few persons delighting in singularities and changes, open and manifest disorder, specially in the external, decent, and lawful rites and ceremonies to be used in the churches." Naturally she turned to the unfailing resource of all malcontents in Church matters—now specially associated with the claim to represent the most Catholic principles and profoundest reference for Church authority—viz. to railing against the Bishops. Her letter to the Archbishop begins with a prolonged scolding of him and his suffragans, which, omitting much verbiage, runs thus: "Altho' our earnest care hath been from the beginning of our reign to provide that by laws and ordinances, consonant to good order, this our realm should be governed . . . in the ecclesiastical policy by officers following one rule and directing our people to obey and live . . . without novelties of rites and manners. Yet for lack of regard had thereto in due time by such principal officers as you are, with sufferance of sundry varieties and novelties, has come this disorder and diversity."

The Archbishop's position was difficult and delicate in the extreme. Manners and prudence, forbade him to tell a lady, and a Tudor monarch, that the real fault lay in the impracticable character of her own personal legislation on ritual, at the "beginning of her reign." She must, however, have had some consciousness of the fact; and sought, in a fashion not unknown

[1] App., Strype, Parker, vol. iii. p. 66; Queen's Letter, Jan. 25, 1564-5.

to the gentler sex, to cover her mortification by " fuming and chiding " (as the Archbishop afterwards expressed it),[1] and throwing the blame on him. He, of course, took the chiding in meek silence, and set himself to the task imposed on him. " We have certainly determined," was her royal word, " to have all such diversities brought to one manner of uniformity through our whole realm." But how ? Uniformity in observance of the Rubric was utterly out of the question. The Queen herself had, during the six years of its existence, tacitly acquiesced in the completely *uniform rejection*, by the clergy, of her own special piece of legislation. Moreover, the Queen's own Rubric was contradictory to the Queen's own Injunctions issued the same year, 1559. The thirtieth injunction on apparel of ministers, " both *in the Church and without*," commands that " they shall use and wear such seemly habits, garments, and such square caps as were most commonly and orderly received in the latter yere of the raigne[2] of King Edward the Sixth." The Injunctions had the authority of the Queen only, without Parliament ; but while the Rubric is, in contemporary documents, generally ignored, they are very frequently referred to as being the law ; *e.g.* Sandys writes to the Archbishop, October 24, 1560,[3] that his people in the diocese of Worcester " go so soberly and decently as they offend no piece of the Queen's Majesty's Injunctions." Reference to them appears continually in visitation articles.

[1] Letter to Cecil, 8th Mar., 1564–5 ; Parker Correspondence, p. 235.
[2] So in the original edition printed by Jugge, " cum privilegio Regiæ Majestatis."
[3] Parker Correspondence, p. 126.

Here, then, was the Rubric—referring for the rule as to apparel of ministers to the second year, and therefore to the First Book of Edward VI., when the vestments, alb, cope, and surplice were authorized—side by side with the Injunctions referring to the "latter year," and therefore to the Second Book of the same reign, when "alb, vestment, and cope" were forbidden, and the surplice only, enjoined.

About 1561, the Bishops seem to have endeavoured to effect a reconciliation between these two contradictory enactments, by a modification of both.

They drew up and agreed upon a series of "resolutions and orders taken by common consent of Bishops" with "Interpretations, and further considerations[1] of the Injunctions until a synode may be had."[2] On the point now in question, these direct "that there be used but only one apparel, as the cope in the ministration of the Lord's Supper, and the surplesse in all other ministrations." On these Interpretations, we are indebted to Mr. J. Parker for bringing out a conclusion which certainly agrees well with the facts, and throws light on much that is otherwise very obscure. He observes[3] "that they were in some way or other accepted and understood to be *the law*" (the italics are his own), "I have every reason to believe, though not emanating from the Crown. They are, no doubt, what Archbishop Parker refers to, in his letter of March 3 (1564–5), as forming the basis of the first draft of the Advertisements which he sent to Cecil." Mr. Parker adds: "I know of no other way

---

[1] Cardwell, Documentary Annals, vol. i. p. 204.
[2] Ibid., p. 205.   [3] Letter to Lord Selborne, p. 98.

to account for the mention only of the surplice and cope, both before 1566 and after, as being the only vestments for the Holy Communion, than that these resolutions were considered to be authorized, and that the alb and chasuble, though not abrogated by any more definite authority than the Archbishop's paper implies, had gone out of use."

As we have seen from Sandy's letter to P. Martyr of April 1, 1560, that the use of alb and chasuble was then unknown to him, they must have "gone out of use" so early, that they can hardly have been used under the Rubric—then only a year old—at all.

Here is one of the few references to the Ornaments Rubric, to be found in the contemporary documents. The Bishops, though they do not expressly mention it, must have had it in their minds; for the series of resolutions, beginning with that which " directs that there shall be used but one only apparel," is headed "concerning the Service Book."

They regarded the Injunctions as modifying the Rubrics. The resolution next following, directs, "That the table be removed out of the choir into the body of the church, before the chancel door, where either the choir seemeth to be too little, or at great feasts of receivings ; and at the end of the communion to be set up again, *according to the Injunctions.*" The Rubric on this point—the same then as now—only directed that "the table, at the Communion time, having a fair white linen cloth upon it," should stand where the "morning and evening prayer" were appointed to be said, whether that place were in the "body of the church, or in the chancel." When the Communion office was not being used, the Rubric left it open for the Holy

Table to remain in the same part of the body of the church, or the chancel, or to be set anywhere else ; *e.g.* in the vestry, with or without covering. The Injunctions,[1] after directing that the taking down of altars, "according to the form of the law therefore provided," should be effected only in an orderly manner, "by oversight of the curate of the church and the churchwardens, or one of them at least," further directed that " the Holy Table in every church be decently made, and set in the place where the altar stood, and there commonly covered, as thereto belongeth, and as shall be appointed by the visitors, and so to stand, saving when the Communion of the Sacrament is to be distributed, at which time the same shall be so placed in good sort within the chancel, as whereby the minister may be more conveniently heard of the communicants in his prayer and ministration, and the communicants also more conveniently and in more number communicate with the said minister. And after the Communion done, from time to time the same Holy *Table* to be placed *where it stood before.*"

This direction for the position of the Holy Table, when the Communion office is not in use, remains to this day, the only documentary authority for the position now so universally adopted, but for which the Rubric, taken as the sole rule of ritual, made, and still makes, no provision.

On this point the Bishops in their resolution take the Injunctions, with modification, as the rule. As to the position of the Holy Table during celebration, they extend the rule of the Injunctions, which limited it to be "within the chancel;"

[1] Cardwell, Documentary Annals, p. 201; and edit. Jugge, *supra*, p. 34.

and limit that of the Rubric—which allowed, and allows, it to be in any case, in any part of the body of the church appointed for saying Mattins or Evensong—to the particular part "before the chancel door;" and to the case in which the chancel might "seem to be too little" for the convenient accommodation of the number of communicants.

So, in their resolution with respect to "apparel" in divine service, they extend the rule of the Injunctions, which would limit it to the surplice, by including the cope; and *limit* that of the Ornaments Rubric by excluding the vestments—alb and chasuble.

We may suppose that this compromise between the conflicting rules came to be, as Mr. Parker observes, "accepted and understood to be the law," the more readily because it represented the practice generally "accepted" by those with whom the practical acceptance or rejection of ministerial apparel must lie, *i.e.* the clergy. It is clear that, while alb and chasuble were rejected by them with entire unanimity, the surplice was received by the great majority, and the cope, though disliked and probably little used by the majority, was still recognized as a lawful piece of apparel.

There seems reason to think that the Queen herself,—whatever her original intention when she caused her Rubric to be inserted in the Service Book,—was early led by the force of facts too stubborn to bend even to her strong will; and probably by the influence of her secretary; to accept the same compromise. It was just what Cecil had himself suggested to the Revisers of the Service Book, viz. " whether, in the celebration of the

Holy Communion, priests should not use a cope besides a surplice" (see p. 22).

With respect to Cecil, we are confronted by the puzzling fact that, under his secretaryship, there issued from the Crown, simultaneously, two contradictory rules for ministerial apparel: the Rubric making the second year of Edward VI.,—and the Injunction making the "latter" year of that monarch,—the standard; both probably passing through his hands. The Rubric must almost of necessity have done so; though, no doubt, that was the expression of the Queen's will, whether Cecil approved it or not. As to the Injunctions, we know that he took part in the drafting of them, if he was not their author. Archbishop Parker, in his last letter, from his death-bed, to the then Lord Treasurer,[1] says, "Whatsoever the ecclesiastical prerogative is, I fear it is not so great as *your pen* hath given it her *in the injunction*." It seems not impossible that this astute statecraftsman—when the Revisers of the Service Book declined his proposal as too much, while the Queen insisted on more—cunningly allowed the contradictory edicts to go forth together, in order, by balancing and directing the conflicting forces, to bring about a resultant compromise. Whether, however, by his design or otherwise, the result seems to have come about. The Bishops adopted the compromise in their "resolutions and interpretations." The Queen, in her own chapel (where, of course, she could always find clergy to carry out her behest), though she adhered for a time to the crucifix as one of the "ornaments of the Church," appears, for "ornaments of the

[1] Parker Correspondence, p. 479.

minister" to have had, not chasubles, but copes. Heylyn, in his glowing account of the state of the Church in her second year[1] describes "how well they" ("cathedral and most of the parish churches" as to ritual) "were precedented in the court itself" with choral services in the Queen's chapel, "by the gentlemen and children in their surplices, and the priests in *copes*, as often as they attended the divine service at the holy altar. The altar furnished with rich plate, two fair gilt candlesticks, with tapers in them, and a massy crucifix of silver in the midst thereof."

But a compromise like this, though "accepted and understood to be law" by the majority of the Bishops and clergy, and even by the Queen herself, could only hold while no attempt was made to enforce it on the minority, who were unwilling to accept it.

Now that the Queen had "certainly determined to have all diversities brought to one manner of uniformity through her whole realm," the matter assumed a different aspect.

The Archbishop charged to execute the royal commands, had to see, not merely what was "accepted and understood to be law," but what law, having coercive authority, there was, by which uniformity could be enforced *in invitos*.

Here he found :—

1. A Rubric having the authority of Queen, and partly not wholly, of Parliament, but which, in its *original* sense, had never been observed by anybody, and was generally ignored, even by its authoress, the Queen herself;

[1] History of the Reformation, Ann. Eliz. Reg. 2, § 7, ii. p. 315. See *infra*, Appendices II. and IV.

2. Injunctions having the authority of the Queen only, yet generally recognized as law, and put in active operation by a machinery of Royal Commissioners; but which, on the burning question of ministerial apparel, prescribed a rule contradictory to that of the Rubric;

3. Resolutions and interpretations by the Bishops, generally "accepted and understood to be *the law*," prescribing a rule of apparel intermediate between that of the Rubric and that of the Injunctions; but for that very reason, incapable of enforcement under either; and having, in themselves, no claim to coercive authority; having never even been published.

This was the legislative chaos, out of which the Archbishop was now commanded by the Queen to evolve order and uniformity; and well scolded because he and the other Bishops, had not already done so.

What he had to do, therefore, before he could enforce uniformity, was to get uniform law made, that could be enforced.

The conclusion of the Queen's letter, scolding ended, afforded a basis for such needed legislation. "Therefore," she says, "we do, by these our present letters[1] require, enjoin, and straitly charge you, being the metropolitan, according to the power and authority which you have *under* us over the province of Canterbury (as the like we will order for the province of York), to confer with the Bishops, your brethren, namely, such as be in the commission for causes ecclesiastical," first to ascertain what "varieties, novelties, and diversities there are in our clergy;" and thereupon to "proceed by *order, injunction*, or *censure*,

[1] Parker Correspondence, p. 225.

according to the order and appointment of such laws and ordinances as are provided by Act of Parliament and the true meaning thereof, so that uniformity of order may be kept."

"Orders or injunctions," having legal claim to obedience, must precede "censures" for disobedience. To this point, therefore, the Archbishop first addressed himself. With his fellow-commissioners, the Bishops of London, Winchester, Ely, and Lincoln, he prepared a draft of "ordinances," which, after perusal by Cecil, was fair copied, and subscribed by them, and again sent to Cecil for the Queen's sanction. Here were fulfilled the conditions for that "other order being therein taken" under the proviso in the Act of Uniformity, "until" which order should be taken, the retention and use of the ornaments of Edward VI. was only provisional. For this the Queen's authority was made statutably sufficient; but she must act "with the advice of her commissioners appointed and authorized under the great seal of England for causes ecclesiastical, or of the metropolitan of this realm."

The advice either of her commissioners, "*or* of the metropolitan" would have been sufficient, but she had the advice of both. All that was needed to make the ordinances legally binding was her own authority sanctioning them. But this, still "fuming," she hesitated to give. The Tudor mind was not yet prepared for the public practical acknowledgment that the "laws and ordinances," by which, "from the beginning of her reign, it had been her earnest care to provide" for uniformity, were such a chaos of contradictions, and much of them so completely a dead letter, that fresh laws and ordinances were necessary for the purpose. Cecil's knowledge of her temper had led him, before the issue of her letter, to "doubt whether the Queen's Majesty will not be provoked to some offence that there is such cause of reformation."[1]

She seems to have clung with feminine generalization and inaptitude for legal distinctions, to the idea that there was *plenty of law*, if those ever-in-fault Bishops would only enforce it; (as, indeed, there was too much to be capable of enforcement), and still more, probably, to the idea that her ecclesiastical prerogative would supply all that could be needed; and that, having in her letter to the Archbishop uttered her *sic volo sic jubeo*, nothing remained for her subjects but implicit obedience; especially if she had herself condescended to "accept and understand to be law," less than she originally intended on the matter of the "ornaments of the church and of the ministers."

There was, besides, a powerful influence at Court favourable to the puritanical party, who not only invoked it, but vaunted of it as won to their side.

"My Lord of Leicester, they say" (writes the Archbishop)[2] "shall move and obtain the Queen's Majesty, and this thing is now done in his absence." Strype[3] prints two elaborate letters to him, to this effect, from Durham—where puritanical proclivities were then strong—one from the Bishop and one from the Dean. The former reminds the favourite, of Mordecai's

---

[1] Letter to the Archbishop, Jan. 15, 1564–5; Parker Correspondence, p. 223.
[2] Parker Correspondence, p. 237.
[3] Parker, vol. iii. App., Nos. 25, 27, p. 71.

exhortation to Esther " when she made *curtesie* to speak for God's people being in danger," as applicable, *mutatis mutandis*, to his own position and influence.

Whatever that influence might amount to, it probably tended to make the Queen more wishful to keep herself in the background, and to let the Archbishop " bear " (as Mr. Parker says) " the brunt of the opposition." He was to perform the part of a modern railway buffer in the collision. He, for his part, was ready to accept the situation, but only on condition that he had the Queen's statutable authority at his back; without that, he knew that his own authority, episcopal or archiepiscopal, would avail nothing. If his hopes of that were overturned, " I am," he writes,[1] " at point to be used and abused ; *nam scio nos episcopos in hunc usum positos esse*. We are the stiles over which men will soonest leap over " (*sic*).

When he sent to Cecil the " book (of ordinances) subscribed by the Bishops conferrers," he wrote :[2] " If the Queen's Majesty will not authorize them, the most part be like to lie in the dust ; " and as they did lie, endorsed by Cecil, " not authorized or published," (and no reason why, made known to him)[3] the Archbishop kept to his resolve to hold his hand, and make no attempt to enforce as law, what he knew was not really law. He tried expostulation with the recusants, on one hand, and with Cecil on the other. Both failing, he wrote to the latter :[4] " For mine own part, I repose myself *in silentio et in spe :*

---

[1] Parker Correspondence, p. 237.
[2] Ibid., p. 234.
[3] Letter to Cecil ; Parker Correspondence, p. 263 ; see *infra*, p. 46.
[4] Parker Correspondence, p. 246.

et fortitudo mea dominus, howsoever the world fawneth or fumeth."

So, for more than a year after the issue of the Queen's letter—which she probably expected would of itself suffice to bring recusants in trembling submission to uniformity—nothing effective was done, and matters only got worse.

But the very "fuming" of the world was tending to bring about the result which the Archbishop was patiently waiting for, *in silentio et in spe.*

At Cambridge, the University of which Cecil was Chancellor, the Fellows and Scholars of St. John's and Trinity, had thrown off their surplices; and much other disorderly conduct prevailed, calling for his interference. His own chaplain resident there, wrote to ask on behalf of the Vice-Chancellor, "by what law he could deprive a man of his living for refusing to wear a surplice?"[1]—a question to which the Chancellor probably found an answer not so ready and complete as he had imagined.

At Court, too, some ventured so far as to preach before the Queen herself, without the habits.

This bold defiance must have helped to open the royal eyes, and those of the Chancellor and Secretary, to see, with the Archbishop, the need of fresh effective legislative "order being taken."

[1] "JOHN WELLS, *to* CECIL:

"It is demanded of Mr. Beaumont (Vice-Chancellor), who is very diligent in observing the order presented by your honour, by what authoritie he can, for not wearing of a surplice, deprive any man of his lyvinge."

Record Office. Calendar of State Papers, Domestic Series, of Reign of Edward VI., Mary, Elizabeth, 1547–1580, vol. xxxix. p. 14.

So, near the end of March, 1565–6, the Archbishop and the Bishop of London were "called to the Queen's presence" to receive in person, from her own lips, the royal commands.[1] These were twofold. She "charged them both, to see (1) *her laws executed*, and (2) *good orders decreed* and observed." The first was only what the Archbishop had often heard before, and knew how little it amounted to; but the second gave him what he had been long waiting for, viz. the Queen's authority and command that "*good orders*" should be, first "*decreed*," then "observed."

What was understood between the Queen and the Archbishop by the "good orders to be decreed," we may gather from a letter which the latter had previously written to Cecil, dated March 12; 1565–6,[2] enclosing again, the "ordinances" of the previous year, and also an open letter addressed to the Queen, of which he says: "This letter, if your honour think it tolerable, I pray you seal it up and deliver it. I hope by the bearer to have some good answer." And previously, "I have written to the Queen's Majesty, as you see. I pray your honour to use your opportunities. And where once this last year, certain of us consulted and agreed upon *some particularities on apparel (where the Queen's Majesty's letters were very general)*, and for that by *statute we be inhibited to set* out any constitutions *without license obtained of the prince*, I sent them to your honour to *be presented;* they could not be allowed then, I

---

[1] Letter to Bishop Grindal, March 28, 1566. Parker Correspondence, p. 273.

[2] Parker Correspondence, p. 262.

cannot tell of what meaning; which now I *send again*, humbly praying that if not all, yet so *many as be thought good*, may be returned with some authority, at *the least way for particular apparel.*"

The "call" into the Queen's presence followed, and was no doubt, the immediate result of these letters from the Archbishop. He had now, once more, placed the Ordinances in Cecil's hands to be laid before the Queen, " humbly praying that if not all, yet so many as might be thought good, might be returned with some authority, at the *least way for particular apparel.*"

We can hardly doubt that Cecil again laid the Ordinances before the Queen; still less that the Archbishop, in his personal interview with her, must have pressed upon her this particular point, to which he attached so much importance; and therefore that it must have been before her when she "charged him to see good orders decreed."

Thus armed at last, with the Queen's authority, the Archbishop lost no time in carrying her royal "charge" into effect. He prepared a new draft of the Ordinances, of which he writes to Cecil on March 28, 1566,[1] "I have weeded out of these articles all such of doctrine, etc., which, peradventure, stayed the book from the Queen's Majesty's approbation." He changed the name from Ordinances to Advertisements; omitted the articles of doctrine; and altered the preface, so as to make the Queen's letter of January 25, 1564-5,—"charging that some orders be taken whereby . . . diversities might be reformed

[1] Parker Correspondence, p. 271.

and brought to one manner of uniformity throughout the whole realm,"—the basis of the "orders now taken." With these exceptions the Advertisements were identical with the Ordinances. They were so, on the point, then, as now, crucial, viz. the "particularities in apparel." On this, they followed the lines of the "Interpretations of the Injunctions" above referred to (p. 35), except that now, the use of the cope was limited to the "ministration of the Holy Communion in cathedral and collegiate churches." The Archbishop clearly refers to the "Interpretations" in his letter to Bishop Grindal of the same date (March 28) as his letter to Cecil, and sent, in draft, at the same time with the book of Advertisements for the Secretary to "peruse with his pen." In this[1] he writes of them as "particular description of orders to be followed, which, as your lordship doth know, were agreed upon among us *long ago*, and yet in certain respects not published."

The Advertisements, therefore, on this point, followed what had long been "accepted and understood to be the law" (see p. 40), and now to be *made binding* law by promulgation under the Queen's authority, expressed in her letter of March 25, 1564–5.

Here I am obliged to part company with Mr. J. Parker, to whom I am indebted for much help in the endeavour to trace the somewhat complicated history of this matter.

Mr. Parker is an advocate of the vestments, and, like most of those who take that side,—following therein Cosin's Second and Third Series of notes,—he slips away from the ground of Church authority and falls back upon Acts of Parliament.

[1] Parker Correspondence, p. 273.

The object of his "Letter to Lord Selborne" is to make it appear that the Advertisements were not State-law, but *only* Church-law; that they were issued by the Archbishop on his ecclesiastical authority as metropolitan; without the authority of the Queen according to the Act of Parliament.

This view is confronted by very strong antecedent improbabilities.

1. It is very improbable that the Archbishop—whose attitude had, up to this point, been very consistently maintained—should here have suddenly changed his front, and done that very thing which, in spite of royal "chiding" and puritanical provocation, he had steadily kept from doing, viz. proceed to an act of *legislation* without the Queen's authority.

2. It is still more improbable that he should have taken this step with the knowledge distinctly present to his mind, that if he had taken it, he would himself have been committing an illegal act. Less than three weeks before, viz. on March 12, 1565-6,[1] he had written to Cecil, " by statute we be inhibited to set out any constitutions without license obtained of the prince." He was entering into a legal conflict with opponents, whose temper and determination he well knew. It would have been the height of folly in him, to attempt to enforce constitutions which could have no coercive force; and the issuing of which in the way Mr. Parker supposes them to have been issued, would have been in direct contravention of statute law as well known to those opponents as to himself.

3. Though the Queen had—under the failure of her ritual

[1] Parker Correspondence, p. 263.

legislation at " the beginning of her reign "—remained passive for a time, it is clear that she had now abandoned that attitude; and that she was very far from being disposed to abdicate her prerogative. From among other evidence on this point we may cite that of one who must have been well acquainted with the circumstances,—Horne, Bishop of Winchester, who was one of the Bishops conferrers, who, with the Archbishop, drafted the original "Ordinances;" and one of those in whose names the Advertisements were finally issued. In a letter to Bullinger—written five years later, August 8, 1571, but clearly referring back to, and including the period and matter now under notice—he writes,[1] "Ecclesia nostra nondum e vestiariis illis offensionum scopulis enatavit quibus primum impegit. Clavum ut scis, *tenet, et adhuc quo vult vertit princeps optima.*" Horne's *primum impegit* and *adhuc vertit* clearly imply that the Queen's imperious will had made itself felt, not only when he was writing, but from the beginning of the vestiarian controversy; and therefore at the time of the issue of the Advertisements, in which he had taken part. That, under such a Queen, not only commanding, but piloting the ship of the State ecclesiastical, the Archbishop should have dared, without her sanction, to employ Wolfe, one of the royal printers under patent,[2] to print, and himself to give official publication to, a set of legislative constitutions on a matter, on which ; not only did the Queen claim to legislate by virtue of her much cherished prerogative ; but had had such authority expressly given her by statute ;

[1] Zurich Letters, App. p. 146.
[2] Typographical Antiquities. By Ames and Herbert, and Dibdin, vol. iv. p. 1.

that, doing this without her sanction, he should have ventured to print on the title-page, "ADVERTISEMENTS . . . by virtue *of the Queen's majesties letters commanding* the same," is an improbability little short of the incredible.

Who can doubt that if the Archbishop, or any other subject, had done this without her sanction, the Queen would at once have caused the publication to be suppressed, and visited the audacious authors with condign punishment? Mr. Parker[1] insists, with the typographical aid of mighty capitals, on the expression in the Archbishop's letter to Cecil of March 28, 1566, "the Queen's Highness will have nedes have me assaye WITH MINE OWN AUTHORITYE"—(so here prints ordinary type)—"what I can do for order." But it is clear from all the circumstances, that the "authority" here spoken of, was not legislative, but executive and judicial; that the Queen chose to have the law put in operation, and carried out by the Bishops; not that she attributed to them authority to *make* law without her sanction. The Archbishop could not have intended by the words "mine own authority," an authority to *legislate*, which; without the royal license and sanction, he so well knew that the clergy were precluded from exercising in general by the statute 25 Hen. VIII. c. 19, s. 1; and which on the now urgent question of "particularities of apparel," had been specially reserved to the Queen, by 1 Elizabeth, c. 2, s. 25.

Mr. Parker's theory is as inconsistent with subsequent history, as with antecedent probabilities. It is inconsistent with the contemporary and early subsequent documents, even as they

[1] Letter to Lord Selborne, p. 45.

appear in the pages of his own "Letter to Lord Selborne," though there accompanied by paraphrases and explanations—often rendering *obscurum per obscurius*—by which he labours to reconcile his theory with them. It seems to me absolutely irreconcilable with these documents as they stand in full in their own places, and without his exegetical apparatus. To point out this in detail, would require more than the hundred pages of his "Letter to Lord Selborne." I will only take an example or two of the documents, and the methods of interpretation to which he is driven in defence of his thesis.

Lord Selborne has printed[1] from a MS. in the Record Office, a letter, dated May 21, 1566, from Grindal, Bishop of London, to the Dean and Chapter of St. Paul's, enclosing the Advertisements, and running thus :—[2]

"After my hartie comendacyons, these are to require and to give you in especiyall charge that wth all convenyent speed, yo^u call before yo^u all and singuler the mynisters and ecclesiastical psōns within yor Deanry of Powles and office, and to prescribe and enjoyne everie of them upon payne of deprivacōn to prepare forthwth, and to weare such habit and apparell as is *ordeyned by the Queenes maiesties authoritie expressed in the treaty intituled the advertisem^{ts}.*, etc., which I send herein inclosed unto yo^u, and in like to injoyne everie of them under the said payne of deprivacon, as well to observe the order of mynistracōn in the church with surples, and in such forme as is sett forth in the saide treatie, as alsoe to require the subscription of every of them to the saide advertisem^{ts}."

[1] Notes on Liturgical Revision into English Church, App. A. p. 74.
[2] State Papers, Domestic, Elizabeth, vol. xxxix. No. 76.

Here, to an ordinary understanding, the Queen's authority seems to be plainly ascribed to the Advertisements, in an official promulgation of them to his Cathedral Chapter by the Bishop of London, who, about two months previously, had, along with the Archbishop, received from the Queen in person the royal command, " to see good orders decreed and observed," which we know (see pp. 46, 47) was speedily followed by the printing and issue of the same Advertisements.

But Mr. Parker is fertile in typographical and other expedients.[1] In his reprint of Grindal's letter he inserts a comma between the words "Queen's Majesty's authority," and the word "EXPRESSED," which he prints in capitals. With this typographical divorce of adjective from noun, he proceeds to argue that the Queen's authority is not ascribed to the "Advertisements sent therein enclosed," but to the Injunctions of A.D. 1559, issued seven years before, and of which Grindal's letter makes no mention.

In his eagerness to get rid of the authority of the Advertisements, Mr. Parker here overlooks the fact that his principal thesis, viz. that the Rubric continued to be *the* law of ministerial apparel, is even more inconsistent with the Injunctions than with the Advertisements. He quotes with inverted commas the words of the thirtieth injunction, which directs that " ministers, etc. . . . should use and wear such seemly habits, garments, and such square caps," adding, without commas, as were commonly received in the reign of Edward VI., which also are words of the injunction ; but which stand with the important

[1] Letter to Lord Selborne, p. 56.

date omitted by Mr. Parker, "received in the *latter* year of the reign of Edward VI." They thus directly contradict the "second year" of the Rubric, and make the practice under the Second Prayer-Book of Edward VI. the standard of ministerial apparel, instead of that under the First. The Queen's authority in the Injunctions was, therefore, opposed to all "ornaments of the minister," except the surplice. So, in the Injunctions, "other order" was "taken by the authority of the Queen's Majesty;" but they failed to fulfil the requirements of the Act of Uniformity, in that the order was not taken "with the advice of her commissioners . . . or of the metropolitan." This defect was supplied in the Advertisements. But this by the way.

The punctuation by which Mr. Parker tries to support his utterly non-natural interpretation of Grindal's letter, is merely his own, not the Bishop's. I have examined the original MS. in the Record Office, and compared it with Lord Selborne's appendix, where it is very accurately printed. Commas are used in the MS. as shown by Lord Selborne ; but there certainly is no comma where Mr. Parker inserts one—between "authority" and "expressed ; " nor is there any indication of a break in the continuity of the clause at that point.

Mr. Parker seems to me equally to fail in his elaborate efforts to reconcile his theory with the other documents, official and unofficial, quoted by Lord Selborne and by himself; or to invalidate Lord Selborne's statement[1] that "no writer of reputation, in any work published before the eighteenth century,

[1] Notes, etc., p. 13.

seems to have suggested a doubt that they (the Advertisements) were, as a matter of fact, authorized by Queen Elizabeth."

I will only add—from much producible—one piece of evidence on this point (not quoted by Lord Selborne or Mr. Parker), from those witnesses whose interest would have led them strongly to side with the view now taken by Mr. Parker; because they were the first to suffer under the authority of the Advertisements, viz. Sampson, who was deprived, and Humphrey, who was driven into reluctant conformity.

In their joint letter to Bullinger, of July, 1566, soon after the Advertisements were enforced by actual deprivation—referring to the liberty that had previously been enjoyed under the mutually contradictory and impracticable enactments on ritual—they write:[1] "*a libertate in quo hactenus stetimus*, discedere, servitutis auctoramentum quoddam esse judicamus;" and they add, as to the then present state of things, " In ritibus nihil est liberum; nec ad hoc a nobis *regia majestas irritata est*, sed aliorum suasu *inducta;* ut *nunc demum*, non quod ecclesiae expedit, sed quod aliquo modo licet, *constituatur*."

Their "*nec a nobis irritata*," was in answer to a caution from Bullinger, in his letter to them of May 1, 1566,[2] "lest this dispute, and clamour, and contention, respecting the habits should be conducted with too much bitterness, and by this importunity a handle should be afforded to the Queen's Majesty to leave that no longer a matter of choice to those who have abused their liberty; but being *irritated* by their needless

[1] Zurich Letters, App. p. 95, Epist. 71.
[2] Zurich Letters, p. 349.

clamours, she may issue her orders, that either these habits must be adopted or the ministry relinquished."

The "*aliorum suasu*" was clearly aimed at the Archbishop. It accords with what he had himself written to Cecil, April 7, 1565,[1] of the Puritanical party, "unrestful they be, and I alone, they say, am in fault. For, as for the Queen's Majesty's part, in my expostulation with many of them, I signify their disobedience, wherein, because they see the danger, they cease to impute it to her Majesty, for they say, but for my calling on, she is indifferent. I only am the stirrer and the incenser."

They were very ready to lay all the blame they could on the Archbishop, and to "impute to her Majesty" as little as possible. But if there had been any foundation in fact, for Mr. Parker's theory, they might have gone much further in that direction. They might have told Bullinger, with truth, that the Archbishop was not only the adviser and instigator, but the actual doer of the legislative Act, by which the liberty which they had hitherto enjoyed, had been changed into a condition, of which they complain "*in ritibus nihil est liberum.*" Their answer to his remonstrance would have been far more complete if they could—as on Mr. Parker's hypothesis they might—have bid him "cease to impute the Act to her Majesty" as they had themselves previously endeavoured to do. But their "inducta ut nunc demum constituatur" clearly shows that they knew the then recent legislative Act to be the *Queen's*.

That they knew this, is even more decisively proved by the submission of Sampson to deprivation, and of Humphrey to

[1] Parker Correspondence, p. 237.

conformity. Had it been otherwise, we cannot doubt that able men as they were, of "unrestful" spirit and strong determination, would have denounced the Archbishop's constitutions as issued in defiance of well-known statute law, and would have flatly refused obedience to them as utterly invalid and illegal.

I will now only call one other "unwilling witness" against Mr. Parker's theory, and that is Mr. Parker himself. At the conclusion of his section on the "History of the Queen's letter of January, 1565," and "why Archbishop Parker issued his Advertisements in 1566,"[1] he puts the question, "Did the Queen ever go so far as to sanction their issue?" and himself gives the answer, "*Possibly she did;*" in three words admitting a possible negative to the thesis, for which his whole letter is an elaborate argument, viz. that they were issued on the Archbishop's "own authority," and without her sanction. He proceeds, as we might expect, to minimise the effect of this admission by adding, "but the evidence mainly rests upon the two or three words in the Archbishop's letter to the Bishop of London, viz. hath charged us, being called to her presence, to see her laws executed;" but he unfairly stops short of the very important words immediately following, "and *good orders decreed.*" These words, though but four in number, and far from being the only evidence, abundantly prove that the Queen's sanction was given to legislative "orders" being "decreed;" or, in the words of the statute, "order" was to be taken by the authority of the Queen's Majesty, with the advice "of her commissioners . . . and the metropolitan." This was done in the Advertisements,

[1] Letter to Lord Selborne, p. 51.

of which, as the chief *adviser*, the Archbishop goes on to speak to Grindal as "these our convenient orders described in these books at present sent unto your lordship."

Probably the Queen had learnt a lesson from the failure of her attempt in the Ornaments Rubric, to legislate independently of the clergy, for the Church. Clearly now, her policy was, that "order" should be taken *through* the proper ecclesiastical authorities, viz. the metropolitans, each in his own province. The same letter of January 25, 1564-5, had concluded: "Therefore we do, by these our present letters, require, enjoin, and strictly charge you, being the metropolitan, according to the *power and authority which you have under us* over the province of Canterbury, (*as* the like we *will order for the province of York*), to confer . . . inquire . . . and proceed by order, injunction, etc."

We see here what the Queen meant when she directed the Archbishop[1] to proceed by his "own authority," viz. "a power and authority" which she deemed him to "have under her" in her cherished capacity as "Supreme Governor." An authority to legislate independently of her—such as Mr. Parker supposes her to have bid him exercise—was surely the very last thing she dreamt of.

That she did, as intimated in the letter of January 25, 1564-5, "the like for the province of York," appears from a letter of Archbishop Parker to Cecil, of April 28, 1566 (soon after the issue of the Advertisements in the province of Canterbury),[2] beginning, "the Queen's Majesty willed my Lord of York to

---

[1] See p. 51.   [2] Parker Correspondence, p. 280.

declare her pleasure determinately to have the order go forward."

The question as to legal formalities, which Mr. Parker supposes to have been required to constitute a "taking order by the authority of the Queen," under the statute 1 Eliz. c. 2, s. 25, is clearly one to be decided by lawyers expert in the construction of statute law. Mr. Parker's attempt to add to his useful historical inquiries, a legal argument, simply proves that he is not a lawyer; and illustrates the rule "*ne sutor ultra.*"

Into that question I will not attempt to enter. My purpose is not to inquire what, as to ministerial apparel, is the "discipline which this realm has received" by Acts of Parliament, but "what this Church has received" by the acts of the clergy.

Seeing, however, that Mr. Parker is so frequently and confidently referred to, as having demolished the validity of the Advertisements; and having myself, gratefully to acknowledge much assistance derived from him, I have felt bound to give reasons for entire dissent from him on this point.

I gladly leave this tedious inquiry, which Mr. Parker's theory as to the Advertisements, has seemed to me to render necessary, and return to a point of agreement with him.

Mr. Parker's conclusion,[1] that the rule laid down in the Bishop's interpretations of 1561, authorizing the cope and surplice to the exclusion of chasuble and alb, was "accepted and understood to be the law"—even before the issue of the Advertisements—is strongly supported by what we know as to

[1] See p. 35.

the destruction of the latter, with other ornaments, as being unlawful.

§ III.—Authorized Destruction of Vestments.

Much peculation and destruction of ornaments of the Church and of the ministers, had, no doubt, taken place, through rapacity of courtiers, sacrilege, and Puritanical violence, in the reign of Edward VI.; and even in that of Mary; as well as in the earlier years of Elizabeth. But, simultaneously with the issue of the Advertisements, the process was carried on, with regular forms of law, and under the direction of the recognized authorities in Church and State. This is shown by the returns from a hundred and fifty churches in the Diocese of Lincoln, printed from the original MSS. in Mr. Peacock's "Church Furniture." Here we find, acting on a royal commission, five or six *commissarii Regii*, headed by the Bishop of the diocese and the Archdeacon of Lincoln. The Bishop was Nicholas Bullingham, one of the "devisers," with the Archbishop, of the Ordinances, and one of those whose names were subscribed to the Advertisements. The Archdeacon, who took the most active part in the whole proceedings, was John Aelmer (so he signs his name), better known as Aylmer, afterwards Bishop of London. It appears that the churchwardens had received orders at his visitation previously held in that year, 1565, old style, to make returns in accordance with the forty-seventh of the Queen's Injunctions of 1559, which directed—

"That the Churchwardens of every Parish shall deliver unto

our Visitors the Inventories of Vestments, Copes, and other ornaments, plate, books, and specially of Grayles, Couchers, Legends, Processionals, Manuals, Hymnals, Portuesses, and such like pertaining to the Church."

The churchwardens appear in this case to have been directed to include in their inventories, all ornaments which had been in their several churches since the death of Queen Mary; and to state what had been done with them. The inventories were exhibited and sworn to, by the churchwardens, on dates ranging from March 17, 1565, O.S., to May 2, 1566, in the presence of one or more of the commissioners who countersigned the documents.

From their returns it appears that the churchwardens had received instructions, at the visitation, as to what should be done with the ornaments, etc., still remaining; viz. which should be destroyed or defaced, as "monuments of superstition," and which retained as still to be lawfully used. Among the former, along with images, and the roodlofts on which they had stood, books of the Latin service, etc., are classed the vestments. Some of these ornaments of the Church and the ministers had been destroyed in the first year of Elizabeth, some in subsequent years, and some only "since Mr. Archdeacon his visitation Anno Domini 1565."[1] To an inventory of April 22, 1566, exhibited before the Bishop and two lay commissioners, in which[2] the churchwardens say "a vestment remayinth (*sic*) in o' church," and speak doubtfully as to some other ornaments, the commissioners add, "The said Churchwardens have to verifie

---

[1] Church Furniture, p. 54. [2] Ibid., pp. 76, 77.

before Maie daie next of the defacing of such things as remaine at this daie unaltered and to certify more certainly for the rest." In a similar case,[1] exhibited before the Archdeacon alone, where he seems not to have been satisfied as to the destruction of a vestment, he has added a note, "Let the Churchwardens see ye defaced." Of the *use* of vestments after the first year of Elizabeth, I cannot find a trace. On the other hand, the copes, though many of them had shared the indiscriminate destruction of the earlier years, were then recognized as lawful ornaments; *e.g.* in an inventory,[2] exhibited before the Bishop, the Archdeacon, and a lay commissioner, though with *lacunæ* in the MS., the churchwardens have written ". . . have a cope in the churche wch wee ar admitted . . . tions to kepe for o^r minster." Here the gap before "tions" may have been filled by "at the visitations." The use of that word in the plural for a single archidiaconal or episcopal act, is, or was, recently common in the vernacular of country places. Or it may have been "by the Injunctions."[3] Certainly the entry "a cope yet remayninge," frequently appears, unchallenged by the commissioners. One zealous pair of churchwardens conclude their inventorie recording how a vestment and other things had been made *awaie* or "defaced" thus :[4] "Item one cope—remayninge in or said pishe, so that wee have no monument of supersticon now remayninge." Another pair, more learned in the law, conclude a similar record : "Item a cope with all thother [5] (*sic*) things

[1] Church Furniture, p. 147.
[2] Ibid., p. 42.
[3] See below, p. 63.
[4] Church Furniture, p. 115.
[5] Ibid., p. 114.

according to thinjunctions remaineth in o' said pish church A"dni 1565." [1]

The reference by these churchwardens to the Injunctions as authorizing the cope, which they must have derived from "Mr. Archdeacon," or other superior, is remarkable. It goes to confirm an observation in Mr. Parker's "Letter to Lord Selborne," p. 60, that the "Interpretations and further considerations" agreed on by the Bishops, were considered as part of the Injunctions. The Injunctions themselves made no mention of the cope. The thirtieth injunction, referring to the "latter year of Edward VI." for the standard of ministerial apparel, would exclude the cope, as it was expressly excluded by the second book of Edward VI., then in force. But the discrepancy is explained by Mr. Parker's conclusion, that the Interpretations "were accepted and understood to be law." The Injunctions, as modified by the Interpretations, were held to authorize the cope, which, if taken by themselves, they would have excluded. On the other hand, the Rubric, modified by the same Interpretations, was not held to authorize the vestments, as it would have done if taken by itself.

The marked distinction made by the Royal Commissioners in their treatment of the vestments, and of the copes, shows that, in directing the destruction of the former they were acting on what they understood to be the law; not actuated by the puritanical spirit which, though it might love vestments less, certainly did not love copes more.

[1] The blending of the article with a following word beginning with a vowel, as here written, is still common in northern dialects.

A like conclusion results from what we know of the two dignitaries of the Church, who were at the head of the Royal Commission for Lincoln.

The Bishop, at the same time that he was directing the destruction of the vestments in his diocese, was acting with the Archbishop in the issue of the Advertisements, which were certainly, in the first instance, directed against puritanism. But he clearly had no conception of the modern theory that they were only intended to enforce a *minimum* of ritual, leaving the Ornaments Rubric as still the rule of *maximum*; when he was depriving his clergy of the wherewithal to conform to that rule, if any of them had wished to do so. If the Queen herself had still been bent on retaining the Rubric in the *maximum* sense, it is hardly conceivable that her own commissioners, acting in her name, could have ventured on so flagrant a violation of it; or that Bullingham at least, could have been ignorant of the royal intention, being—as he must have been—in communication on the matter with the Archbishop, who was then receiving her commands from the Queen in person.

Of the Archdeacon of Lincoln, Strype gives us this account:[1] —"Mr. Aylmer lived in great reputation, and was one of the Queen's Justices of Peace for the County, and one of her Ecclesiastical Commissioners, being an active and bold man as well as wise and learned. Here, in short, as his office led him, he first purged the Cathedral Church of Lincoln, being at that time a nest of unclean birds; and next in the county by

[1] Life and Acts of Aylmer, p. 14.

preaching and executing the commission, he so prevailed, that not one recusant was left in the county at his coming away."

On a general review of his life and acts, Strype gives him this character :—[1]

"In the discharge of his duty, the Bishop was very conscientious and exact, and spared for no pains being naturally an active and stirring man; and so he was particularly in his episcopal function, one part of his diligence consisted in *pressing due conformity unto the laws and orders of the Church established*, and that because he thought it the best bulwark to secure from Popery. This was the cause he spared neither Papist nor Puritan. Whereby *he drew upon himself the hatred of both; but especially that of the Puritan appeared most visibly against him* setting Martin Marprelate loose upon him, and giving him all the trouble they could any other way, as we have seen in part of the foregoing history."

The "foregoing history" shows him in frequent legal conflict with many leading Puritans; as President of the Ecclesiastical Commission pronouncing sentence of imprisonment on Lord Rich, the notorious Thomas Cartwright, and others; and of deprivation, on Cawdry, whose famous case (says Strype)[2] created him and others with him work for four or five years after. One ground of Cawdry's deprivation was "for not conforming himself in the celebration of the divine service and administration of the Sacraments, but refusing so to do; though" (continues Strype) "indeed for the most part he did conform himself to the book, only leaving out the cross in

[1] Strype, Life and Acts of Aylmer, p. 184.   [2] Ibid., p. 85.

baptism and the ring in marriage." Strype gives many other instances of Aylmer's strictness in the enforcement of conformity.

A man so much engaged in legal conflict, and whose acts were so calculated to stir opposition from right and from left, was not likely to escape recriminations of the kind which it is now the fashion to bandy against the Bishops, as being themselves law-breakers. Strype's narrative shows that he did not escape them. Now, on the supposition that the Ornaments Rubric, in its *maximum* sense, was still the law, Aylmer was specially open to the retort, that he had been conspicuous, not only as a law-breaker himself, but as a cause of law-breaking in others; that he, who was so strict in enforcing on the clergy exact conformity to the Book of Common Prayer, had, by his destruction of the vestments, rendered it impossible for the Lincoln clergy at least, to conform. But though many things were alleged against him, I have found no trace of such a charge as this. Men's minds were stimulated by the conflicts of the period to seize upon legal and other points which might tell for their own side, and against their opponents, as Cosin's was by his conflict with Peter Smart, and as many minds are now. That so obvious a point should not have taken against Aylmer, is an indication confirming the conclusion from much other evidence, that the Rubric, as directing the use of the vestments, was known not to be the law of the Church.

The order on which the Lincolnshire churchwardens acted, was given at Archdeacon Aylmer's visitation, before the issue of the Advertisements. It was, therefore, not founded upon them, but upon what had been previously "accepted and understood to be the law," viz. the rule prescribed in the Interpretations agreed upon by the Bishops.[1] This rule was, as we have seen, a compromise between the conflicting directions of the Injunctions and the Rubric. The Interpretations had never been formally enacted. The rule, therefore, though accepted and understood to be law, *could not have been* coercively enforced. The vestments seem to have had no friends to defend them, and so the question of State-law, then existing with respect to them, was not raised.

But when the Queen had, in her letter of January 25, 1564–5, proclaimed herself "certainly determined to have all diversities, etc., brought to one manner of uniformity through her whole realm," it became necessary to replace the existing chaos of conflicting directions, by a clear and consistent enactment by which uniformity could be enforced against recusants. For this purpose, the Advertisements were devised. On the question of ministerial apparel, they followed the rule of the Interpretations with one exception, viz. whereas these directed generally "that there be but only one apparel, as the cope in the ministration of the Lord's Supper, and the surplice in all other ministrations;" the Advertisements limited the use of the cope to cathedral and collegiate churches. For this change there were obvious reasons. In many places the copes had perished in the indiscriminate destruction of the earlier years. To replace, and permanently to maintain, such costly ornaments might have been beyond the means of many parishes. More-

[1] See above, p. 35.

over, there is no doubt that the use of copes was distasteful to a considerable number of the clergy. Under these circumstances it would have been difficult, if not impossible, to enforce that general uniformity on which the Queen had set her mind. Hence, probably, the limitation in the Advertisements of copes to cathedral and collegiate churches, which might generally be expected to have means to provide and maintain them. With this limitation the Advertisements agreed with the Interpretations in recognizing the cope as a lawful *kind* of ministerial apparel.

But that the vestments were unlawful in kind, is clearly shown by the way in which they were dealt with after the issue of the Advertisements. In 1571 we have "injunctions[1] given by the most venerable father in Christ, Edmonde (Grindal), by the providence of God, Archbishop of York, Primate of England and Metropolitan, in his metropolical visitation of the Province of York, as well to the clergy as to the *Laytie* of the same Province, Anno Do : 1571."

Under a head, "For the Laytie," the seventh injunction directs—

"That the Churchwardens and Minister shall see that antiphoners, masse bookes, Grayles, Portesses, Processionals, Manuelles, Legendaries, and all others of late belonging to their Church or Chapell, which served for the superstitious latine service, be utterly defaced, rent and abolished. And that all *Vestments*, *Albes*, Tunicles, Stoles, Phanons, Pixes, Paxes, Hand-belles, Sacring-bells, Sencers, Crismatories, Crosses,

[1] Second Report of Royal Commission on Ritual, App. p. 411.

Candlestickes, Holywater stocks or Fattes, Images, and all other reliques and monuments of superstition and ydolatrie, be utterly defaced broken and destroyed."

Now, on the supposition that Queen Elizabeth's Rubric, directing that "the minister at the time of the Communion and at all other times in his ministration shall use such ornaments, etc.," continued still in force as including the use of vestments and albes, how are we to understand the action of Archbishop Grindal in directing them to be destroyed? Was it mere puritanism, reckless of the law of Church or State? There are, in this case, reasons like those which rendered that explanation insufficient in the case of the Bishop and the Archdeacon of Lincoln; like them, but very unlike the desires of the puritanical party.

Grindal spared the copes. These are conspicuously absent in his exhaustive list of ornaments to be destroyed. Moreover, he, as Bishop of London, had taken a still more active part than the Bishop of Lincoln in the issue of the Advertisements. In these same injunctions he insists, as Aylmer, both when Archdeacon and when Bishop, did, but as the Puritans certainly did not, on conformity to the Prayer-Book. His second injunction "for the clergie" orders that they "shall at all times, requisite and convenient, duly and reverently minister the two holy Sacraments, that is to say, Baptism and the Lord's Supper, commonly called the Holy Communion, *according to such order, as is set forth in the booke of Common Prayer*, and administration of the Sacraments."

Grindal clearly must have deemed this direction to be

consistent with his other direction, that vestments and albes should be destroyed. He must, therefore, have come to the conclusion that the meaning of the Rubric had, in some way or other, been so modified that "the order set forth in the book of Common Prayer" did not then require the use of vestments and albes.

Thus far, Grindal might, like the Lincoln Commissioners, be following the Interpretations which the Bishops and clergy had accepted and understood to be the law.

But Grindal's formal issue of metropolitical injunctions for the clergy and laity of the northern province, goes beyond what can be thus explained on the hypothesis, that Grindal's destructive injunction was neither in accordance with the will of the Queen, nor with the law of the realm.

We are again brought face to face with difficulties of the same kind as, but still greater than, those which beset Mr. Parker's theory as to the Advertisements.

Unless Archbishop Grindal's injunctions either were issued with the royal assent and license; or were merely declaratory of the existing law of the realm; his issuing of them must have brought him into collision with both. On this point, the one question, What was the existing law of the realm? resolved itself into the other, What was the will of the Queen? The Act of Uniformity, 1 Eliz. 2, s. 25, made the period during which the ornaments of the second year of Edward VI. were to "be retained and be in use" to depend on two things—the "authority of the Queen" and "the advice of her commissioners" "or of the metropolitan." We know what the advice of the

Royal Commissioners, including the Metropolitan of the southern province, was in this case. It was embodied in the Advertisements. If these were issued "by the authority of the Queen's Majesty," then, so far as they prescribed a rule different from that of the second year of Edward VI., "other order was taken;" and the period during which the former order was in force, was, to the extent of the difference, brought to an end.

On this supposition Grindal's issue of his injunctions is perfectly intelligible. He was carrying out, not only what the Bishops and clergy had, from the time of the Interpretations "accepted and understood to be the law;" but also the determination which the Queen had come to, and proclaimed in her letter of January 25, 1564–5, "to have all diversities brought to one manner of uniformity through her whole realm;" by directing the destruction of ornaments which might be the occasion of diversity.

But on the hypothesis, that the Queen had refused to authorize the Advertisements because she still wished that *all* the ornaments of the second year of Edward VI. should "be retained and be in use," we have, in Grindal's injunctions, the second in rank of those whom she regarded as "principal officers" acting under her; to whose predecessor in that office she had referred, in the words of that same letter to Archbishop Parker: "We strictly charge you, being the Metropolitan, according to the power of authority which you have under us over the province of Canterbury, as the like we will order for the Province of York"—we have the metropolitan of York using the power of authority which he had under her "to destroy, throughout that Province, the ornaments which, on that hypothesis, she wished to be retained, and had, in her Rubric, ordered that "the Ministers should use."

It is to be remembered (see p. 50) that this year, 1571, in which Grindal's injunctions appeared, was the same in which Horne, Bishop of Winchester, wrote to Bullinger, touching the same subject-matter:—"vestiariis illis offensionum scopulis. Clavum ut scis tenet, et adhuc qua vult vertit, Princeps optima."

It is just conceivable that the Queen might not have known what her commissioners did in the Lincoln Diocese; though this is extremely unlikely, from the nature of the case; from the keen personal interest which the Queen took in the matter; and from the general disappearance of the vestments, which renders it probable that similar action was taken in other dioceses of the southern province. But that she should remain ignorant of an act so public as the issue of Grindal's injunctions is utterly inconceivable. As if purposely to "beard the lion(ess) in her den," Grindal had his injunctions printed, not, as one might have expected, at York; but in London, by William Seres, who held the Queen's license—*cum privilegio ad imprimendum solum.*[1]

How far Grindal was the man whom—

"Non vultus instantis tyranni
Mente quatit solida,"—

the man thus daringly to defy a Tudor queen, touching a matter which she had taken under her special personal direction; and on which, the law of the realm followed her will,—may be gathered

---

[1] Typographical Antiquities, by Ames and Herbert and Dibdin, vol. iv. p. 195.

from an incident which occurred this same year, 1571, during his metropolitical visitation, thus narrated by Strype:[1] "About August this year, the Archbishop of Canterbury had some business with his brother, our Archbishop; for, being old friends and fellow-commissioners in ecclesiastical matters, this distance brake not off their friendship. Now he sent to him a book of articles and discipline, seasonable for his intended visitation; the same, I make no doubt, with that entitled, *Liber quorundam Canonum Disciplinæ Ecclesiæ Anglicanæ*, which is still extant in Sparrow's collection. It was drawn up in a late synod by the Archbishop of Canterbury and some other Bishops; to which all the Bishops of the Province subscribed, either by themselves or proxies; but *wanted the Queen's confirmation to authorize the observation of it; though she were privy to it, and did not dislike it,* yet that did not seem sufficient to secure against a *premunire*, those Bishops or others that should go about to enjoin it; *and these were the fears of Archbishop Grindal,* to whom his brother the other Archbishop, sent it, with that intent to bring it in practice in his Province, as it was made for that other. As for the book itself he declared he liked it very well; . . . but he *made hesitation*, saying 'that he stood in doubt whether the articles contained in it had *vigorem legis, i.e.* the virtue of a law; unless they had either been concluded on in a synod and after ratified by her majesty's royal assent *in scriptis* (fine words,' added he, 'fly away as wind,' [meaning as it seems of the Queen's verbal approbation] 'and would not serve us if we were impleaded in

[1] Life and Acts of Archbishop Grindal, p. 246.

a case of *premunire*), or else were confirmed by Act of Parliament.' But the Bishop of Canterbury, in a letter, soon after written, told him that he was in more fear than he trusted would follow; for that he and the Bishop of Ely had so ordered the matter with the Queen, that, seeing there was no new doctrine in the book, [but only matters of discipline and good order,] she seemed to be contented; and that, therefore, if it were repealed hereafter, there would be no fear of a *premunire* matter; as he might better satisfy himself, by considering the statute. Thus Archbishop Parker wrote to him to put the book in force. *But Grindal did not care to go upon such uncertainties.*"

In this contemporaneous and closely parallel case, Grindal exhibits none of that heroic defiance of the Queen and the law of the realm, which the hypothesis that she was still maintaining her Rubric intact, requires; but rather a timid caution as to both, which goes far to render the hypothesis incredible. Though "he liked very well" the "Book of Canons" drawn up in the Synod of the southern province, and unanimously adopted by all the Bishops there, "he made hesitation" to enjoin it in his own province, because it had not her Majesty's royal assent *in scriptis.* Though assured by his brother Archbishop that he and the Bishop of Ely had so ordered the matter with the Queen . . . that there would be no fear of *premunire* matter, he still declined "to go upon such uncertainties."

Before a man who *declined* to enjoin canons thus supported, for want of the Queen's formal assent *in writing*, ventured, himself to issue an injunction in direct opposition to what it is now the fashion to speak of as "the plain grammatical sense" of her Rubric, he must have been well assured that "other order" *had been* "taken by authority of the Queen's Majesty with the advice of her commissioners," which we know she had in the Advertisements.

That Grindal was following the Advertisements, and not merely the understanding as to the Interpretations appears from this: that while his injunction for destroying unlawful ornaments, passes over the cope as lawful in kind, in his "Articles to be inquired of," in the same metropolitical visitation, No. 7 he asks,[1] in connection with the "use in the ministration of the Holy Communion of any gestures, rites, or ceremonies not appointed by the Book of Common Prayer," and other *illicita*, "whether your person (*sic*) curate or minister doe wear any cope in your *Parish Church* or chappell."

He thus recognizes the difference created by the Advertisements, from the law as previously understood, in that these limited the use of the cope to cathedral and collegiate churches.

The part which Grindal had taken in the issue of the Advertisements, and his personal interviews with the Queen, had given him the best opportunities of knowing, at the time, her mind, and all that was done in the matter. The contrast between his decisive action under the Advertisements and his hesitation as to Archbishop Parker's "Book of Canons" shows that he must have been well assured, that, in the former case, he had Queen and law with him. From this and all the other

[1] Second Report of Commissioners on Ritual, p. 408.

circumstances, the inference seems very strong that such was, in fact, the case; and that the Advertisements had become the law of the realm, superseding, to the extent of the difference, the Rubric as enjoining the vestments, and the Injunctions as forbidding the cope.

When so much turned upon the will of the Queen, it is important to note her conduct after the issue of the Advertisements and of Grindal's injunctions. Though ready enough to find fault, there is no trace of her finding any, in either of these cases.

As to the first named, that she approved of Grindal's conduct in that and other matters, appears in her raising him to the metropolitical see of York; and giving him, in his first year there,[1] (instead of her frequent gift to Bishops, viz. a scolding) "a standing cup, double gilt, in token of her good affection to him." After his more prominent—and if not in accordance with the law and her will—daringly defiant action in his injunctions, I find no appearance of change in her sentiments towards him. He certainly continued on the best of terms with Cecil, and was, in 1575, further elevated to the see of Canterbury. He did afterwards incur her displeasure, and was sequestered and confined to his own house for six months; but that was in a matter not at all connected with his injunctions, viz. the increase of the number of preachers, and the "exercises" for training them in the interpretation of Holy Scripture (a thing not unneeded now), which Grindal supported in a firm and temperate letter to her; but which she suppressed with a strong hand, therein

---

[1] Strype, Grindal, p. 242.

verifying Horne's words, *clavum tenet et quo vult vertit princeps optimâ.*

That Grindal's injunction directing vestments, etc., to be destroyed, was in accordance with the law as accepted previously by the Bishops and clergy, and then by the Queen and the realm—is proved by the fact that the action was not only unchallenged by the royal authoress of the Rubric, but was continued by him as Archbishop of Canterbury in Metropolitical Visitation Articles for that province, printed by Seres,[1] 1576; by Aylmer, Bishop of London, in Articles, 1577;[2] by successive Archbishops of York, and their suffragans; and the Queen's Commissioners; as long as any trace of the existence of the vestments, could be found.

This last has been shown from the original documents, and visitation books in the registry at York, by the learned northern antiquary, Canon Raine, in his paper, "Vestments: what has been said and done about them in the Northern Province since the Reformation." London: Rivingtons, 1866. He found, dated September 30, 1577, the articles of inquiry issued within Darlington *ward*, Durham, by Richard Barnes, the Bishop of that see, and others, his associates,[3] "the Queen's Highnes' Commissioners for the hearing, ordering, and determining of causes ecclesiastical within the saide diocese of Durham, and everie parte therof, by virtue of her highness saide commission to them under the great seale of England directed." One article

---

[1] Grindal's Remains: Parker, Soc., p. 156.
[2] Second Report of Royal Commission on Ritual, p. 418.
[3] Vestments, etc., p. 15.

asks, "whether your several parishe churches and chappels be furnished with and have all necessary bookes and other furniture requisite, and which by the lawes and injunctions ought there to be had; and whether *that any be knowen or suspected to have or kepe any restmentes, tunicles,* mass bookes, grailes, etc., images, crucifixes, pixes, *paxes,* or any other suche cursed and execrated abhominable monumentes of superstiction poperie and idolatrie."

Another inquiry of these Royal Commissioners under the great seal of England, is somewhat amusing, as indicating that the sixteenth century might, sometimes, present a spectacle resembling what I have myself witnessed more than once in the latter part of the nineteenth century, viz. that of a clergyman in knickerbockers.

They inquire, "whether there be any persons, vicars, curates, or other person ecclesiastical that wear laic apparell, great ruffs, *great bumbasted breches,* skalinges, or scabulonious clokes, or gownes after the laic fashion and contrarie to the *Advertisements* and Injunctions."

These last words show that the Royal Commissioners recognized the Advertisements originally issued for the Southern province, as having the force of law in the Northern.

Canon Raine notes here, "These articles are taken from a MS. in the York registry. They direct obedience to the Common Prayer-Book, as well as to the Advertisements and Injunctions."

He further found that "on the day after these articles were issued, Oct. 1, 1557, Bishop Barnes promulgated a number of synodal injunctions to the clergy and churchwardens of his whole diocese."

As in the Lincoln case, so here. We have the Royal Commissioners, as representing the realm, acting in concert with the Bishop, as there with the Archdeacon, representing the Church.

Canon Raine continues: "In these he lays down a list of furniture implements and books 'requisite to be had in every church, and directs that the parsons, vicars, and curates at ministracion of sacraments wear clean and comlie surplesses.' It is worthy of remark that the comperts [1] for several years after this visitation are preserved, and that in them there is no allusion to the use of vestments. In 1578 Archbishop Sandes held a metropolitical visitation adopting as it seems almost entirely the injunctions of his predecessor (Grindal). Some vestments were traced at one of the parishes in Cheshire. The compert which I copy as an instance, runs '*Grappenhall*, Thos Sutton hath in his hands a cope of read velvit, imbrodered with gold; a cope of white sattin; a vestment of sattin bridges, blacke and grene; a vestment of sackclothe, another of sackclothe; a banner of green sarcenet; III. canstricks and II. crosses, latelie belonging to the church; the which they presented to my L of Chester, who appointed it to be sold for the churche's use, but yet it is not.'" Here the Bishop of Chester had appointed the vestments, etc., found in the hands of a private person, and the copes, as being unlawful in a parish church, to be *sold* for the church's use, *not* restored to it.

Canon Raine continues: "In 1590 Archbishop Piers inquired, principally as it seems for form's sake, 'whether all

---

[1] Comperts = charges in Ecclesiastical Courts proved to be true after due investigation.

copes, vestments, albes, tunicles, etc., and such like reliques of popish superstition and idolatry be utterly defaced and destroyed,' and in three cases some of these prohibited articles were found. After this *there is no trace of them whatever in any of the injunctions or comperts* throughout the north of England."

That this search for, and destruction of, the vestments—continued until no further trace of them could be found—should have been formally ordered, not only by successive Archbishops and Bishops in their public visitations, without a word of disapproval from the Queen, or anybody else; but also by her own " commissioners under the great seal of England, for the hearing, ordering, and determining of causes ecclesiastical,"—if these vestments were still legally included among the ornaments, which her own Rubric ordered that the " minister at the time of Communion should use,"—is, to my mind, simply incredible. But if—in consequence of the Queen's determination " to have all diversities, varieties, etc.," brought to one manner of uniformity throughout her whole realm—the " other order " contemplated by the Act of Parliament, which her Rubric, on the face of it, professed to follow, had, in fact, been " taken by her authority with the advice of her commissioners, etc. ;" and the temporary sanction given by that act to the use of vestments, thus withdrawn ; the whole course of the proceedings, becomes intelligible and consistent; instead of, as it is otherwise, an inexplicable puzzle. The conformity to the Book of Common Prayer frequently insisted upon, both by Bishops and Royal Commissioners, was then, conformity to the book as modified by the other order which had been taken.

A review of the evidence on this matter, during the reign of Elizabeth, forces upon me these conclusions—

1. That from the time when the Queen's Rubric appeared in the Prayer-Book, the use of the vestments with that book, was rejected by the clergy with such entire unanimity, that; though many vestments were then in existence; no evidence that any of them were ever used with the English book, has been found;[1] while there is much that points strongly to the opposite conclusion.

2. That the rule "agreed upon" by the Bishops in their interpretations (see p. 33)—"that there be used but *one only apparel*, as the cope in the ministracion of the Lord's Supper, and the surplesse in all other ministracions," excluding, therefore, the vestments—was accepted by them and the clergy, though not unanimously, yet so generally that it soon came to be, as Mr. Parker says, "understood to be the law;" and was acted by the Queen's commissioners in the Lincoln Diocese, where the records have been preserved; and probably in the other dioceses of the southern province, where the records and the vestments, alike have disappeared.

3. That when the Queen had proclaimed her determination "to have all diversities, etc., brought to one manner of uniformity throughout her whole realm;" and, after hesitating for more than a year to admit practically that "the laws and ordinances," by which, "from the beginning of her reign, it had been her earnest care to provide for uniformity," could not be uniformly enforced,—as, indeed, they contradicted one another,

---

[1] The one exception at Durham really proves the rule (p. 92).

—became convinced of the fact; then "other order was taken by her authority with the advice of her commissioners" in the Advertisements, by which the rule of apparel, previously agreed upon by the Bishops, (except as to the use of the cope in parish churches,) and generally accepted by the clergy, became the law of the realm; and was thenceforward acted upon; both in the purely spiritual visitations of Archbishops, Bishops, and Archdeacons; and in those of a mixed nature created by the Queen's commission under the great seal.

It has not been, and is not now, my purpose to go into the question of the law of the realm. That is a question to be decided by judges learned in the law. But I have been forced to inquire into the proceedings connected with the Advertisements, because, without some light upon these, the history of the matter during the reign of Elizabeth is absolutely unintelligible. I will only observe—as it is now the fashion to say that the Privy Council judgments have interpolated a *not* into the rubric—that the *not* as to the vestments, was read into it, during the reign of its Royal Authoress, by her own commissioners, "for the hearing, ordering, and determining of causes ecclesiastical ... by virtue of her Highness's commission to them under the great seal of England directed;" as well as by the Archbishops and Bishops in their respective visitations. The former, representing the realm, and the latter the Church, took the most effectual order that the vestments should *not* be used, by directing that they should be destroyed whenever they could be found.

§ IV.—Canons of 1604-5.

After the accession of James I., the question as to the discipline on ministerial apparel received by the church, was dealt with in the canons agreed upon by the Bishops and clergy of the Canterbury Convocation in A.D. 1604,[1] and of the York Convocation A.D. 1604–5.[2] In these we have the action of the purely clerical legislature, deliberating under license from, and its acts subsequently sanctioned by, the Crown; but without any interference on the part of the secular Parliament. They present one of the few instances, in which the two provincial synods,—after full separate deliberation on the same subject matter,—came to conclusions so consentient, that the result may fairly be deemed the act of "the sacred synod of this nation, in the name of Christ, and by the King's authority assembled," which is declared by the 139th canon, then passed, to be "the true Church of England by representation."

As to ritual, the fourteenth canon orders that[3] "singuli ministri studiose observabunt instituta ritus et ceremonias omnes quæ in dicto libro (precum publicarum) præscribuntur, tam in sacris scripturis legendis ac precibus recitandis quam in administrandis sacramentis, *absque ulla sive materiæ sive formæ additione aut diminutione*, respectu vel concionis, vel *alterius causæ cujuscunque*."

[1] Wilkins, vol. iv. p. 380.   [2] Ibid., vol. iv. p. 428.
[3] Sparrow Collection, p. 275.

Now, on the hypothesis that the Rubric which directed that "the minister at the time of the Communion, and at all other times in his ministration, shall use such ornaments in the church as were in use by the authority of Parliament in the second year of King Edward the VI.," was still in force as including *all* the ornaments mentioned in the first book of Edward VI., what was the position of the parochial clergy under this canon? It peremptorily insists on precise conformity to the ritual of the book. It expressly forbids any deviation from that ritual, either by addition or diminution; either in the direction of a *maximum* or a *minimum*. Therefore, referring back, according to the hypothesis, to the first book of Edward VI., the parish priest, (if he got sight of that book) would find the direction, that " on the day and at the time appointed for the ministration of the Holy Communion, the priest that shall execute the holy ministry shall put upon him the vesture appointed for that ministration, that is to say a white alb, plain, with a vestment or cope ;" and the further direction that any priests assisting the celebrant, shall " have upon them the vestures appointed for their ministry, that is to say albes with tunicles." How were the parish priests of 1605, to carry out the ritual, thus, on the hypothesis, directed by Rubric, and made strictly imperative, " without any diminution" by the canon? We have seen that vestments, albes, tunicles, and, in parish churches, copes, had, during the previous reign, been destroyed so completely, that the researches of a learned antiquary,—who has specially studied the original ecclesiastical documents of the northern province,—could find "no trace of them whatever in the injunctions or comperts throughout the north of England," later than 1590. There is every reason to believe that they had disappeared still earlier, in the southern province, where we find earlier records of their destruction. How, then, were these costly vestments, copes, etc., to be, first, provided throughout England; and, afterwards, maintained in each parish? The fifty-eighth of these canons directed that "a decent and comely surplice with sleeves should be provided at the charges of the parish, *communibus parochianorum impensis comparabitur.*" But no such provision was made for the cost of vestments, albs, tunicles, or copes. This must be borne, not *communibus parochianorum impensis,*—unless as purely voluntary offerings,—but by the parish priest himself, in order to conform to the canon and the Rubric thus interpreted. Does common-sense allow us to believe that the Upper Houses of two Convocations, deliberately intended to impose such a burden on the parochial clergy; or that, if they had been so unreasonable, the two Lower Houses (that of York after some eight months' time, for consideration), representing, however imperfectly, the parochial clergy themselves,—would have accepted the burden "*unanimis eorum consensu et assensu?*" [1]

The hypothesis here, as elsewhere, leads us *ad absurdum.*

That the Rubric was not thus interpreted is further proved by the direction of the fifty-eighth canon:[2] "Ministrorum quilibet, dum vel publicas preces recitat, vel *sacramenta administrat,* aliosve ecclesiæ ritus peragit, decente et congruo *superpelliceo eoque manicato induetur.* . . . Quotquot vero ex ministris

[1] Wilkins, vol. iv. p. 428.   [2] Sparrow, p. 296.

gradum aliquem in academia susceperunt, ii inter sacra peragenda superpelliceis suis adjicient et caputia singulorum gradibus convenientia." Any parish priest preparing to celebrate Holy Communion—which must surely be included in the *dum sacramenta ministrat*—and comparing this canon with the fourteenth on the hypothesis that, by its requirement of strict conformity to the ritual of the Book of Common Prayer, it referred him back to the Edwardian Rubric; and there finding himself ordered for the same ministration, to put on him a white alb, plain, with a vestment or cope,—must exclaim with Cosin, in his First Series of Notes, "I would fain know how we should observe both canons."

Ingenuity, stimulated by modern controversy, has devised two solutions for the difficulty, which Cosin left unsolved; as on the hypothesis originated by him, it was, indeed, insoluble.

1. To read somewhere into the fifty-eighth canon an "at least;" and to understand it as merely sanctioning the toleration of a *minimum* of ritual. But if the ritual of that canon be regarded as a diminution from that of the Prayer-Book, the use of it would be a direct violation of terms of the fourteenth: "Singuli ministri studiose observabunt, *ritus et ceremonias omnes* quæ in dicto libro præscribuntur, *absque ulla* sive materiæ sive formæ . . . *diminutione* respectu . . . causæ cujuscunque."

Further, if the fifty-eighth canon had been intended only to sanction the use of the surplice as a *minimum*, surely the framers would have indicated the intention by some such mode of expression as they had already used in the twenty-fifth: "In cathedralibus et collegiatis ecclesiis, cessante cœna dominicâ, *satis erit* tempore divinorum *superpelliceis duntaxet uti.*"

But there is no approach to this, in the fifty-eighth canon. Its terms are absolutely imperative.

2. Some of the learned in vestiarian lore,—delighting to pick a hole in a passage in the Privy Council judgment touching on the difficulty of reconciling the directions as to apparel, mentioning only the surplice, which occur so frequently in visitation articles, &c., simultaneously with the requirement of strict conformity to the Prayer-Book, on the hypothesis that the book required vestments and albs,—have maintained that the surplice might be used *along with* those vestments; and have cited mediæval authority to that effect. On this view, the priest desirous to "observe both canons," when preparing to celebrate, would have (as, I suppose, the close-fitting alb must, for physical reasons, be worn under the loose surplice) to put on first, alb; second, surplice; third, if a graduate, his hood; fourth, vestment, or cope; unless the order of three and four were interchanged. Surely the hypothesis which would lead to such a result, reduces itself wholly, and tends to bring the ritual of the most solemn of services perilously near, *ad absurdum*. A *superpelliceum idque manicatum* would be the very opposite of *congruum* for such a use. Moreover, the addition of surplice and hood to the supposed requirements of the Rubric, would be a direct violation of the *absque ullâ additione* of the fourteenth canon.

The Book of Common Prayer had been republished by James I., without reference to the Convocations, "as lately explained in some few points by His Majesty's authority" (canon eighty), but with Elizabeth's Rubric as it stood in her book. The canons are incapable of any reasonable reconciliation with that Rubric, taken as directing the use of vestments, albs, and tunicles; but they are in exact accordance with the "other order taken" in the Advertisements. The first part of the fifty-eighth canon, directing the use of the surplice, and making the cost chargeable to the parish, is *taken, word for word, from the Advertisements.* So also is the substance of the twenty-fourth canon, with express reference to them.

The Advertisements directed that—" In the ministration of the Holy Communion in Cathedral and Collegiate Churches the principall minister shall use a cope with gospeller and epistoler agreeably."[1]

The twenty-fourth canon runs:—" Per cathedrales omnes et collegiatas ecclesias sacram cœnam in festis solemnibus administrari volumus, nounumquam per episcopum, siquidem prœseus extiterit, nonnunquam vero per decanum, quandoque etiam per canonicum, vel prœbendarium (ministrum ibidem maxime eminentem) eundemque decenti capa amictum ac adjutum ab evangelii et epistolæ lectoribus *juxta admonitiones in septimo Elizabethæ promulgatas."*

Here, the two provincial synods of 1604 and 1605, expressly recognize the authority of the Advertisements, and frame their own canons in accordance with them. We have seen[2] that the Advertisements in turn, followed what had previously been "accepted and understood to be the law" by the clergy, viz. the rule agreed upon by the Bishops in their

[1] Wilkins, vol. iv. p. 248. Sparrow, 124.   [2] See above, p. 48.

"Interpretations," which made cope and surplice the "only apparell" to be used under the Service Book. In the one point on which the Advertisements differed from the Interpretations, viz. the limitation of copes to cathedrals, etc., it is probable that the former followed what had been the general practice of the parochial clergy. Mr. Parker puts the question, "Were copes in common use?" and answers, "I think not."[1]

We have seen (p. 75) that the same rule was acted upon in those "archidiaconal and episcopal visitations" (which I observe the president of the English Church Union, in his address of June 21, 1881, kindly sent to me by you, speaks of (p. 5) as "really ambulatory synods") when they directed the destruction of vestments, albs, and tunicles—and, after the time of the Advertisements, in parish churches—copes. That they directed this destruction, while, at the same time, they insisted on strict uniformity and conformity, to the Book of Common Prayer, clearly proves that they did not interpret the Rubric as requiring the use of the ornaments which they ordered to be destroyed. And, now, we find the same phenomena in one of the most—if not absolutely the most—complete and formal legislative acts of the whole "Church of England by representation," of which we have any record. If they received Elizabeth's Rubric reproduced by James I. as modified (1) by Elizabeth's Injunctions, issued simultaneously with it, but which, taken by themselves, contradicted it as to all ornaments of the minister except the surplice; (2) by the Interpretations agreed upon by the Bishops about two years later, which prescribed cope and surplice as the

[1] "Letter to Lord Selborne," p. 102.

only ministerial apparel; (3) by the Advertisements which followed the same rule, but limited the cope to cathedrals;—the action of the Bishops and clergy is intelligible, and consistent throughout the period. But on the hypothesis that the Church's rule of ritual, was to be found in Elizabeth's Rubric, taken barely, without any regard to contemporary and subsequent interpretation; but only with *backward* reference to the first book of Edward VI.; the action of the Bishops and clergy, both in Synod and out of Synod, is absolutely incomprehensible.

§ V.—The Vestments at Durham.

I pass on some two and twenty years, and come to the one solitary instance during three centuries from the appearance of the Ornaments Rubric, in which evidence that the vestments were actually used, has been produced, viz. the Durham case. Of this we have two accounts from Cosin's pen.

1. In his answer to the House of Lords[1] to "the declaration and impeachment exhibited by the Commons upon the complaint of Peter Smart," 1641, he said that, "at his first coming (to Durham) he found two open fashioned vestments to be there usually worne, of which by the late dean's appointment one large cope was made. Defendant, who was then absent, had no hand in ordering it, or directing on what part thereof the story of Christ's passion should be placed."

Fuller says: "The Doctor is charged to have set up in the

[1] Acts of High Commission, Surtees Society, p. 219.

Church of Durham a marble altar, etc., with the appurtenances, namely, a cope with a crucifix, and the image of Christ with a red beard and blew cap."[1] The Surtees editor adds, "This subject is peculiar to the chasuble. The cope thus converted from two ancient vestments, is still in the Dean and Chapter's library."

2. It appears[2] that there is, in the chapter books at Durham, the following entry in Cosin's handwriting, dated June 12, 1627, among the Acts of the Chapter: "It is further agreed that the three vestments and one white cope now belonging to the vestry of this church, shall be taken and carried to London to be *altered* and *changed* into fair and large copes *according to the canons and constitutions of the Church of England*."

There are some not very important discrepancies in these two accounts. There might be some lapse in Cosin's memory, in the thirteen years which intervened between the contemporary entry in the chapter book, and his defence to the House of Lords, as to the number of vestments, etc.

But, however that might be, his answer to the Lords shows that Cosin—from whose Notes originated the view taken up by several later writers, that the vestments were still sanctioned by Act of Parliament—did not attempt to maintain that view before the House of Lords. He merely cleared himself from personal responsibility for the use of the vestments at Durham, as *having begun* before his coming there; and for the particular way in which the figures embroidered upon the vestments, were

[1] Church History, xi. p. 173.
[2] Cosin's Correspondence, Surtees Society, vol. i. p. 170. Note.

transferred to the copes. His entry in the chapter book, shows that he then deemed the vestments *not* to be in accordance with "the canons and constitutions of the Church of England," till they were "altered and changed into copes."

When the vestments had come again into use at Durham, does not appear; but from what we have seen (pp. 43, 75) as to the character and conduct of, at least, one Dean and two Bishops of Durham in Elizabeth's time, it is highly improbable that the vestments were then in use. Be that as it may, it is clear that Cosin, whose name has been, more than any other, invoked as the *insigne præsidium* of the use of vestments, was a party to the act which terminated the use at Durham, on the ground that such use was *not* in accordance with the "canons and constitutions of the Church of England."

§ VI.—CONVOCATION OF A.D. 1661.

Were, then, the canons and constitutions of the Church of England, which required the Durham vestments to "be altered and changed into copes," repealed by what took place in the Convocation of 1661?

It is not, I think, alleged that any more direct and formal repeal of the canons of 1604-5, took place in 1661, than was involved in the retention of the Rubric, with certain alterations from the form in which it stood in the Prayer-Books of Elizabeth and James I.

In my former letter (p. 3) I spoke of the Rubric as being

retained, with only verbal alteration conforming it to the Statute instead of to the Prayer-Book of Elizabeth. In your letter you "entreat me to reconsider that statement." In making the statement, I was following what seemed, and, after full reconsideration, I must say, still seems to me, the best authority, viz. the words used respecting those and other alterations, by the Convocation which made them. I have before me a "Facsimile of the Black Letter Prayer-Book, containing manuscript alterations and additions made in the year 1661, out of which was fairly written the Book of Common Prayer annexed to the Act of Uniformity, 13 and 14 Car. II. c. 4;" and which was found, June 1870, in the same press in the Victoria Tower, with the "fairly copied" book which had been "annexed" to the Act. Mr. Parker says: "It is clear that this book was the official copy of the Convocation," and he therefore calls it the Convocation (*i.e.* official) copy, 1661. It represents the form in which the results of the revision, were laid before Parliament.

On two leaves inserted between the MS. preface and the printed title-page, are two MS. lists in the hand of Sancroft (who acted as secretary throughout); one headed "alterations;" the other "additions;" giving the "old readings" in parallel columns with the "new." The list of "alterations" is followed by the note:—"These *are all* the *material alterations*, the rest are *only verbal*, or the changing of some rubricks for the better performance of the service, or the new moulding of some of the collects." The alteration in the Ornaments Rubric is *not* included in the list of which Sancroft writes, "these are *all* the material alterations." The alternative words, "or the changing of some rubricks for the better performance of the service," are not applicable to the changes which were made in this Rubric. These are excluded from the list said to contain "all the material alterations," and left among the "rest which are only verbal." Surely this is equivalent to a positive statement by the Convocation itself, that it deemed the alterations it made in this Rubric *not* "material," but "only verbal."

You say,[1] "Whereas the old Rubric, as it stood in 1603, concluded with 'according to the Act of Parliament at the beginning of this book,' they erased those words—for what other conceivable purpose than to show that they sought no other authority for their standard than that which was inherent in themselves?"

May I point out that to attribute to such a motive the erasure of the words, "according to the Act of Parliament, etc.," involves, under the circumstances, a serious question of good faith.

Parliaments have always been very jealous as to any attempts to legislate independently of themselves. The Parliament of 1662 was, under the influence of the reaction, specially favourable to the clergy. The House of Commons in that year negatived—though only by a majority of ninety-six to ninety [2]—the question, "whether debate shall be admitted to the amendments made by the Convocation in the Book of Common Prayer, and sent down by the Lords to this House." But, at the same time, it claimed the *right* which it had thus waived, by affirming a resolution "that the amendments made by the Convocation, and sent down

---

[1] Supr. p. 12.   [2] Parker, Introduction, p. 471.

by the Lords to this House *might, by order* of this House, have been debated."

If the clergy in Convocation intended by the erasure of the words "according to the Act of Parliament, etc.," to assert, as I understand you to say, an authority inherent in themselves to *legislate* on the matter in hand, independently of Parliament; the alteration was, from the *Parliamentary* point of view, the most important of any then made. But this alteration was laid before Parliament in a form equivalent to a declaration that it was not a "material," but "only a verbal" alteration. It was, on the supposition, in fact, smuggled through Parliament under cover of a false pretence. I feel sure that you will not be disposed to attribute to the clergy in Convocation an intention, and an act, so dishonourable.

But we have the reason for this alteration given in two very important documents.

1. One which Mr. Parker[1] calls "Cosin's Corrected Copy, 1640–61," and describes as "A series of corrections and alterations (chiefly in Bishop Cosin's handwriting) in a printed Prayer-Book of 1619, but these corrections are further amended in another hand, which is undoubtedly that of Sancroft." The original is in Cosin's library at Durham; and the corrections, which were not embodied in the present Prayer-Book, have been printed from it by the Surtees Society.[2] As this book contained many erasures, another seems to have been prepared, which Mr. Parker[3] calls

---

[1] Parker, Introduction, p. 93.
[2] Cosin's Correspondence, vol. ii. p. 39.
[3] Introduction, p. 96.

2. "Sancroft's Fair Copy, 1661," and describes, "A fair copy of those of the above-named corrections, which have not been subsequently erased. The MS. is *wholly* in Sancroft's handwriting, and written in a Prayer-Book of 1634."

The original is in the Bodleian. Mr. Parker gives reasons for thinking that it represented the result of the committee's revision, and that as such "it was read out, certainly to the Upper House, and probably to the Lower House of Convocation." Sancroft appears to have acted in a double capacity— as secretary to the Revision Committee, and to Convocation itself. He had, therefore, the best opportunities for knowing why the alterations were made.

Both in "Cosin's Corrected Copy" and in "Sancroft's Fair Copy," immediately after the altered Rubric, is written, in Sancroft's hand, "These are the words of the Act itself," with, in Cosin's copy, the reference "v. supra," and in Sancroft's "§ penult ut supra." The reference is clearly to the Act of Elizabeth, which was ordered to be, and was, in fact, reprinted at the beginning of the book of 1662. The "§ penult ut supra" refers to the last clause but one (sect. 25) of the Act of Elizabeth.

The Rubric, as it stood in the Prayer-Books of Elizabeth and James I., did not exactly follow the words of the Act. The purpose of the alterations made in 1661 was to bring its wording into conformity with "the words of the Act itself." So far was it from breaking the Rubric loose from the Act, that it brought the two into closer connection.

As to the words, "according to the Act of Parliament set at

the beginning of this book," Mr. Parker[1] observed that, even in the Elizabethan rubric, they "seem to be somewhat redundant," because, practically, the *substance* " of what is given at the beginning of the book is here given also, so that the reference is not at all needed." Still more was this the case, when the alteration had brought the wording of the Rubric into accordance with that of the Act. It was therefore very natural that the reference to the Act, should be struck out as superfluous.

A further reason against the view, that the purpose of the clergy in Convocation was to assert "the authority inherent in themselves," appears from the fact that they did *not* make an alteration which they might have made, and which was needed if that had been their purpose. They retained the words "by the authority of Parliament." I must ask you to forgive me if I say that the explanation given in your letter to these words, seems to me wholly inadequate. You say,[2] "In the Ornaments Rubric its (Parliament's) authority is mentioned merely as a date, *e.g.* Pontius Pilate in the creed." Surely those words involve much more than a mere date. The date would have been quite as distinctly marked if the Rubric had said " such ornaments, etc., as were in this Church of England in the second year of the reign of Edward VI."

We might then have understood that the ornaments were, at that date, in the Church, by the Church's inherent authority. But the words, as they stand, surrender this. They transfer the source of authority from the Church to Parliament, and reduce the Church to the mere *locus in quo* "the authority of

---

[1] Introduction, p. 344.   [2] Supr. p. 13.

Parliament" was exercised. The English Church has often been charged with Erastianism; but I venture to say, that there is not to be found in all the other authorized formularies of the Church, so much Erastianism as is concentrated in the few words of this Rubric, which is now taken as the battle-cry of those who claim to be the special champions of the Church against Erastianism.

I think those who are now fondly looking back to that second year of King Edward VI. as a "golden hour" of the English Church, can hardly have well considered what was done by the authority of Parliament in that year.

Whether the first book of Edward VI. was ever submitted to Convocation, is a question on which the evidence (the records having been destroyed in the great fire) is not very conclusive.

However that might be, it is clear that any action of Convocation in the matter, if such there were, was utterly ignored in the Act 2 & 3 Edward VI. c. 1.

The preamble recites that, owing to the inconvenience arising from the use of divers forms of Common Prayer, as the "use of Sarum, York, Bangor, and Lincoln, and 'besides the same, now of late much more divers and sundry Forms and Fashions that have been used in the Cathedral and Parish Churches, . . . the King's Majesty, with the advice of his most entirely beloved uncle, the Lord Protector, and other of his Highness' Council' . . . had appointed the Archbishop of Canterbury and *certain of the most learned and discreet Bishops* and other learned men of this realm . . . to draw and make one convenient and meet

Order Rite and Fashion of Common Prayer and Administration of the Sacraments."

This body was clearly not Convocation—which would necessarily have included *all the Bishops*—but the Royal Commission which sat at Windsor, in May, 1548.[1] The place of meeting marked its connection with the Court rather than with Convocation.

The preamble further recites "the which at this time, by the aid of the Holy Ghost, with one uniform agreement, is of them (the Commissioners, *not Convocation*) concluded, set forth, and delivered to his Highness, to his great comfort and quietness of mind in a book entitled 'The Book of Common Prayer,' etc.

"Wherefore the Lords Spiritual and Temporal, and the Commons in this present Parliament assembled, considering

(*a*) "As well the most *godly travail of the King's* Highness, of the Lord Protector, and of other his Highness' Council, in *gathering and collecting* the said Archbishop, Bishops, and learned men together,

(*b*) "As the godly prayers, orders, rites, and ceremonies in the said Book mentioned,

(*c*) "And the considerations of altering those things which be altered, and retaining those things which be retained, in the said Book,

(*d*) "But also the honour of God and great quietness, which by the grace of God shall ensue upon the one and uniform rite and order in such common prayer and rites and external ceremonies to be used throughout England, etc., . . . do give his

[1] Parker, Introduction, p. 22.

Highness most hearty and lowly thanks for the same, and humbly pray that it may be enacted . . .

"That all and singular ministers in any Cathedral or Parish Church shall be bounden to say and use the mattins, etc., in such form and order as is mentioned in the same Book, and none other or otherwise.

"That if any manner of Parson, Vicar, or other whatsoever minister shall refuse to use the said Book, . . . or *shall use* wilfully and obstinately standing in the same, *any other rite, ceremony, order,* form, or manner of mass, openly or privily, or mattins, etc., *than is mentioned and set forth* in the said Book, . . .

"And shall be thereof lawfully convicted, according to the laws of this realm, by *verdict of twelve men,* or by his own confession, or by notorious evidence of the fact, shall lose and forfeit, For his First Offence, the profit of one of his spiritual benefices arising in one whole year, and also suffer *imprisonment* for *six months.*

"For his Second Offence, shall suffer *imprisonment* for one *whole year,* and also shall therefor be *deprived, ipso facto, of all his spiritual promotions;* and if convicted a Third Time, shall *suffer imprisonment during his life.*"

It appears, then, that the considerations on which Parliament based this piece of legislation were :—

1. Deference, not to the judgment of Convocation, or even of the Archbishops, Bishops, and other learned men, but to the *travail of the King and his Council in gathering and collecting* the said Archbishop, etc.

2. Parliament's own judgment on

(b) "The godly prayers, rites, orders, etc.

(c) "The consideration of altering those things which be altered, and retaining those which be retained; and

(d) "The honour of God and great quietness expected to ensue upon the one and uniform rite and order in such common prayer and rites and external ceremonies."

Of Convocation, the Church, or the authority thereof, not a word is said.

Such were the grounds on which and such the manner in which the ornaments of the Rubric were "in the Church by the authority of Parliament in the second year of Edward VI."

What were the courts by which offences alleged to be committed against the Act, were to be heard and determined?

By sect. 3 it is enacted, "That all and every Justices of Oyer and Determiner or Justices of Assize, shall have full power and authority in every of their open and general Sessions to hear and determine all and all manner of offences that shall be committed or done contrary to any article contained in this present Act within the limits of the Commission to them directed, to make process for the execution of the same, as they may do *against any person* being *indicted before them of Trespass*," i.e. with a *Jury of twelve forty shilling freeholders*.

Sect. 4 provides, "That all and every Archbishop and Bishop shall *or may* at all time and times at *his liberty and pleasure* join and associate himself by virtue of this Act to the said Justices of Oyer and Determiner, or to the said Justices of Assize, at every of the said open and general Sessions to be holden in any place within his Diocese, for and to the inquiry hearing and determining of the offences aforesaid."

But the presence of the Archbishop or Bishop was simply a matter of his "liberty and pleasure." The accused could not demand it, nor was the trial invalid without it.

Sect. 11 provides, "That the *Mayor of London, and all other Mayors, Bailiffs, and other Head* Officers of all and singular *Cities, Boroughs,* and Towns Corporate within this realm . . . to which the Justices of Assize do not commonly repair, shall have full power and authority by virtue of this Act to inquire hear and determine the offences aforesaid and every of them, yearly, within fifteen days after the Feast of Easter and Saint Michael the Archangel, in like manner and form as the Justices of *Oyer and Determiner* might do."

If this clause had been still in force, it would seem that Mr. Mackonochie and Mr. Pelham Dale, might have been tried by the *Lord Mayor*; and Mr. Green by the *Mayor of Manchester*.

As an additional lash to the whip for clergy who should " use any other rite, ceremony, order, form, etc., than is *mentioned* and set forth in the said Book," the two last sections provide,

Sect. 12, "That all and singular Archbishops, Bishops, and every of the Chancellors, etc. . . . shall have full power and authority by *virtue of this Act*, to inquire in their visitations, synods, etc., to take accusations and informations of all and every the things above-mentioned . . . and to punish the same by admonition, excommunication, sequestration, or deprivation, etc., in like form as herebefore hath been used by the *King's Ecclesiastical laws.*"

Sect. 13 provides, "That whatsoever person offending in the premises shall for the *first offence* receive punishment of the ordinary, having a testimonial thereof under the said ordinary, shall not for the same offence be convicted before the Justices, and likewise receiving for the said *first offence*, punishment by the Justices, he shall not for the same offence *eft soons* receive punishment of the ordinary."

It is to be observed that the authority of the Archbishops and Bishops to inquire in their visitations, synods, etc., of the things above-mentioned, and to punish the same by admonition, excommunication, etc., was treated, not as inherent in their spiritual office but, as conferred upon them by the Act of Parliament. They "shall have full power and authority by virtue of this Act."

What would those who refuse to plead before Lord Penzance, or the Judicial Committee, have said to proceedings taken under "The Public Worship Regulation Act" of the second year of King Edward VI.?

By the Act 1 Elizabeth, sect. 2—of which the Ornaments Rubric, as it stands in the present Prayer-Book, was part of one proviso—the procedure and penalties of the second year of Edward VI. were re-enacted. Under this Act also, a clergyman who should "use any other rite, ceremony, order, form, or manner of celebrating the Lord's Supper, or mattins, etc.," was liable to be tried by a judge and jury at the assizes, as *any one indicted for trespass would have been;* and if convicted a second time, to suffer imprisonment for a year, and to be deprived *ipso facto* of all his spiritual promotions; and on a third conviction, to "suffer imprisonment during his life."

To such penalties, so to be enforced, if the Rubric, taken by itself, were the law of ritual, every priest was liable who should have celebrated the Lord's Supper *without* an "alb and a vestment or cope." Yet, in fact, for three hundred years from that time, there is not a single case on record in which a parish priest is known to have celebrated *with* alb and vestment.

I, therefore, feel justified in repeating what I ventured to say in my first letter to you (p. 2), that the Ornaments Rubric was an attempt at legislation, *circa sacra*, by authority purely secular, steadfastly resisted by the Church.

To return to the question now before us.

Did the Bishops and clergy in the Convocation of 1661, intend—by *leaving* the Ornaments Rubric with the alterations made, in the Prayer-Book—to reverse all that had been done under the Rubric, by the Bishops and the whole clergy, during the hundred years of its existence,

(1) By the "Interpretations agreed upon by the Bishops," and "accepted and understood to be law" (see p. 33) by the clergy, with such unanimity that no instance in which a parish priest used chasuble and alb during the period, has been found;

(2) By the action of Archbishops, Bishops, and Archdeacons, in their visitations, directing vestments, albs, etc., to be destroyed wherever they could be found (see pp. 66, 75);

(3) By the most formal act of "the Church of England by representation" in the synods of 1604 and 1605, enacting

canons twenty-four and fifty-eight; which specifically direct what the ministerial apparel of the clergy should be, not only without mention of chasuble and alb, but so as to be irreconcilable with the use of those vestments (see pp. 81, 86)?

If the Convocation of 1661 intended, by the alterations made, to bring about so material a change in the practice of the Church, it is difficult to give an explanation consistent with fair dealing and good faith, of the exclusion of these alterations from the list laid before Parliament as containing "all the material alterations"[1] (see p. 91).

But were the alterations themselves, calculated to carry out the purpose attributed to this Convocation?

1. We observe that the form of the Rubric was made less imperative. Elizabeth's Rubric was a direct command to the priest. "The minister at the time of the Communion, and at all other times in his ministration, *shall use* such ornaments, etc."

The Rubric, as altered in 1661, is merely a proviso taken from the Act of Uniformity, that the "ornaments . . . shall be retained and be in use." It is not a command addressed to the minister, or to anybody in particular. No doubt, the use of the "ornaments of the minister" could only be made by the minister; but the "retaining" of them, rather belongs to the churchwardens, as custodians of the church goods.

Now, considering that the positive command, that "the minister at the time of the Communion, and at all other times in his ministrations, *shall use*, etc.," had stood for a hundred

---

[1] The exclusion is quite intelligible, if no alteration from existing practice, was intended.

years, confronting every minister each time he opened the Prayer-Book to say mattins—and yet no parish priest had ever been known to conform to it in respect of chasuble and alb, and none to have been molested for such nonconformity; considering that the Rubric had been so long and so completely a dead letter, there was surely small need to make it *less* imperative. Nobody had obeyed it, and it had hurt nobody. If the Convocation of 1661, intended to change this dead letter into a living rule of practice, ordinary adaptation of means to an end, required that they should take measures to make the disregarded rule more, rather than as, in fact they did, less stringent.

A discussion has recently been going on among those who think that this Convocation of 1661 intended to revive the use of the vestments, as to whether such use is, now, imperative or optional. The latter view seems to find most favour, and is certainly, in practice, very largely acted upon. We have, weekly, before our eyes, much difference in the usage even of those of the clergy who deem the vestments to be legal; to say nothing about the many who do not. *Non nostrum est tantas componere lites.* I will only observe, that if the Convocation of 1661, contemplated, and intended to bring about, such a result, it is, here again, difficult to regard their mode of dealing with Parliament, as fair or even honest. They had before them a Rubric referring to, and based upon, the Statute 2 & 3 Edward VI. That statute was in the strictest sense what it was entitled, viz. "An Act for UNIFORMITY of Service and Administration of the Sacraments throughout the Realm." It was passed expressly to remedy the evils, real or supposed, arising from diversity in religious rites and ceremonies. It forbade, under pain of imprisonment for life, any minister to use any other rite or ceremony than those mentioned in the book.

The Rubric was originally taken with modifications from, and was, by the Revisers, being verbally conformed to, another Act for Uniformity, 1 Elizabeth, c. 2, passed to enforce the same purpose, under the same penalties, with respect to another Prayer-Book. That book was now under revision in order to be "annexed" to a third act for the Uniformity of Public Prayers and Administration of the Sacraments, and other Rites and Ceremonies, etc. (13 & 14 Car. 2, c. 4). This last enactment was based on a preamble reciting, *inter alia:*—"Now in regard that nothing conduceth more to the settling of this nation (which is desired of all good men) nor to the honour of our Religion, and the propagation thereof, than an *universal agreement in the public* worship of Almighty God, and to the intent that *every person within this Realm may certainly know the rule to which he is to conform in public worship and administration of the Sacraments* . . . be it enacted," etc. "That all and singular ministers . . . shall be bound to say and use Morning Prayer, and in such order and form as is mentioned in the Book annexed, etc."

Such was the purpose of Parliament. If the Convocation of 1661, contemplated and intended to bring about, or even to permit, such a wide diversity as we now witness, under the Rubric which—though they made it less directly imperative than Elizabeth made hers—still retained the imperative forms, " the ornaments shall be retained and be in use; they were leading Parliament to do just the opposite to what it intended to do, by what really amounted to a false pretence. They were inducing it to enact *diversity* under the disguise of words taken from one Act for UNIFORMITY, referring to another, and to be inserted in a third.

Surely it is more in accordance with charity, and with common sense, to regard the Bishops and clergy of the Convocation of 1661, as honest men of ordinary endowments; than as gifted with prescience, penetrating more than two centuries into the future, but *deceivers of their contemporaries.*

2. If the Convocation of 1661, intended to revive the use of chasuble and alb, the word "retained," then introduced from the Act of Parliament into the Rubric, was, as has often been observed, strangely inappropriate. Those vestments had been so systematically sought for, and wherever found ordered to be destroyed; both in episcopal and archidiaconal visitations; and in those of Queen Elizabeth's commissioners; that for seventy years no trace of them had been found in any parish church in the northern province (see p. 77). If any specimens of them existed, it was as rare curiosities. Some few might have been secreted in the private houses of those who adhered to the Roman obedience and ritual. I have heard of one, and only one such, which is preserved in the "Pro Cathedral" at York, and used at great functions in that and occasionally in other churches of the same obedience. In the one solitary instance in which they are known to have been used with the English service since the date of the Rubric, they had been "altered and

changed into copes" under an order written by Cosin, who, above all others, has been supposed to favour the revival.

When the churchwardens of 1662 procured, as they were required to do, the revised Prayer-Book, and read the direction—specially addressed to them as custodians of the goods belonging to the Church,—" such ornaments shall be retained," they would have been surprised and much perplexed, if they had been told that the "ornaments" they were to "retain," were ornaments not then known to exist; or to have existed during the current century, except in the cathedral of Durham; and that there, they had been "retained," only as material converted into a different kind of ornament.

To the parish priest the perplexity would have been enhanced by the consideration, that the ornaments, not having been "retained" by the churchwardens of the previous century, must, in order to "be used," first be *obtained* at his own cost.

If Convocation intended that chasubles and albs should be *obtained* and used, they could hardly have taken more effective means to disguise their meaning, and cause perplexity, than those they did take. They found in Elizabeth's Rubric the words, "the minister shall use such ornaments, etc.," but they erased these words, and substituted " such ornaments, etc., shall be *retained* and be in use."

It seems to me that, under the then existing circumstances, to apply these words to chasuble and alb, would have been contrary to the usage of the English language, and physical possibility.

Only existing ornaments could be retained.

It is physically impossible that things should be " in use," which are not in existence.

Johnson gives five definitions for the verb " To retain." 1. To keep; not to lose. 2. To keep; not to lay aside. 3. To keep; not to dismiss. 4. To keep in pay; to hire (as in to retain counsel). 5. To withhold; to keep back; not in use.

According to none of these definitions, can the participle " retained" be predicated of things non-existent, except in a purely subjective sense; as " retained in memory;" which is clearly incompatible with the context.

To make the Rubric applicable to alb and chasuble in 1661, would have required two interpolations. It should have stood *all* " such ornaments, etc.," " shall be retained," *or replaced* " and be in use."

The proviso in the Act of 1559, clearly referred to the identical ornaments which had remained from the second year of Edward VI. It directed that these should " be retained and be in use until further order should be therein taken," etc.

Queen Elizabeth—in her attempt to convert this temporary proviso as to ornaments then existing, into a permanent rule for the minister—changed the words " such ornaments shall be retained and be in use," into " the minister . . . shall use such ornaments," etc. This imposed, on the minister, an obligation to replace such ornaments as might be lost or worn out. But in 1661, it was notorious that the ornaments existing in 1559, had all been destroyed, and never replaced. When, with this fact patent before their eyes, the Revisers of 1661, deliberately erased Elizabeth's words, and substituted those of the proviso, it seems to me that, crediting them as we must, with knowledge of their mother tongue, we can only understand them to have meant that " *such* ornaments," etc., should " be retained and be in use," as, by reason of their continued existence, were capable of being "retained and in use ;" viz. the surplice in parish churches, and, perhaps,[1] the cope in cathedrals, etc.

3. The Revisers did, however, retain from Elizabeth's Rubric a few words not found in the Act, but with a very significant omission. In the first book of Edward VI., alb and vestment were the vesture appointed for the ministration of Holy Communion. Accordingly, Elizabeth's Rubric ran—" the minister *at the time of the Communion*, and at all other times in his ministration, shall use such ornaments," etc. The Revisers of 1661, kept the words " at all times of their ministration," though not contained in the Act, but they erased the words " at the time of the Communion." Now, if that Convocation intended to revive the use of alb and chasuble, it is very strange that they should have erased the reference to the particular office to which those vestments were appropriated ; while they retained the direction making " the ornaments of the ministers " *homogeneous* " for all times of their ministrations."

---

[1] If strictly construed, the erasure of the words " at the time of the communion," and "other," while the words "at all times of his ministration," only were retained, might be taken as repealing the provision of the twenty-fourth canon, for use of the cope for Holy Communion in cathedral and collegiate churches. But the evident desire to avoid any disturbance of the *status quo*, renders it more probable that the case of cathedrals, as comparatively exceptional, was a *casus omissus* from the purview of the Rubric, and left to the canons.

But this alteration was exactly suitable for the retention of the *status quo*, in which, under sanction of the Advertisements; the canons of A.D. 1604–5; the constantly repeated articles of inquiry in episcopal and archidiaconal visitations (including those of Cosin himself as Archdeacon);[1] the unbroken practice of the parochial clergy during the hundred years of the Rubric's existence; the use of alb and chasuble had been rejected, and the surplice taken as the ornament of the ministers, sufficient for "all times of their ministrations."

It is then very unlikely—

1. That if the Convocation of 1661 intended to bring the clergy to conform to the use of chasuble and alb, which they had neglected, if not refused, to use under Elizabeth's Rubric, they would have erased the direct command "the minister shall use";

2. That if Convocation intended to bring about the use of *new* vestments like those which had been, for all practical purposes, non-existent for seventy years, they should have introduced the word "retained";

3. That if they intended to revive in parish churches, the use of vestments specially appropriated to the celebration of Holy Communion, they should have struck out the mention of "the time of the Communion."

What the Revisers of 1661 did, was to erase from Elizabeth's Rubric all the alterations, by which she had vainly endeavoured to convert the temporary proviso of her Act for Uniformity, into

[1] Cosin, Works, vol. ii. p. 15; and Correspondence, Surtees Society, vol. i. p. 13.

a permanent rule for the clergy, retaining from her, only the words "at all times of their ministrations," which suited the existing use of the surplice for all ministrations.

It is to be remembered that Convocation *had no power* to alter the Act of Elizabeth, which was still to be reprinted at the beginning of the book with the new Act. If the Convocation had altered the Rubric in any other way than it did; or had expunged it altogether; the proviso would still have remained in the Act prefixed to the book. By bringing the Rubric into verbal conformity with the proviso, Convocation was doing all that in it lay, to maintain the *status quo*, which had existed as long as the Rubric itself.

The Convocations of 1604 and 1605, had accomplished the same results, by other means, under the different circumstances in which they were placed. James I. had claimed, by virtue of the royal prerogative and the second proviso of the Act of Elizabeth, authority to "take[1] further order for, or concerning any ornament, righte, (*sic*) or ceremony appointed or prescribed in the Book of Common Prayer;" and that, "his" pleasure known therein either to "the commissioners for causes ecclesiastical, . . . or to the metropolitan," "further order should be taken accordingly."

On this ground, "understanding that there were in the said book certayne things which might require some declaration and enlargement by way of explanation," he had required the Metropolitan and the Bishops of London and Chichester to "take some care and payns therein," and had "received from

[1] Cardwell, "Conferences," pp. 217, 218, 224.

them particular things in the Book declared and enlarged by way of explanation." These, "by virtue of the statutes and by his supreme authoritie and prerogative royal," ... he "did fully approve allow and ratify;" and directed the Archbishop to "command his printer Robert Barker newly to print the said Communion Book with all the said declarations and enlargements, etc."

The book being thus revised, and conformity thereto enjoined by royal proclamation, the Convocations had no power to alter anything in it.

But they had the royal license to make canons.

By the eightieth canon they directed the churchwardens to procure *librum publicarum precum nuper in paucis explanatum ex auctoritate regiâ . . . sumptibus parochianorum;* and, by the fourteenth, enjoined strict conformity to it, *absque ulla sive materiæ sive formæ additione vel diminutione.* They thus accepted the book, and with it, Elizabeth's Rubric. But they made it clear, by the fifty-eighth and the twenty-fourth canons, in what sense they accepted the Rubric, viz. according to the "other order" taken in the Advertisements, which the fifty-eighth canon followed verbally, and the twenty-fourth substantially, with express reference to them. This was the first time the Rubric was ever received by the clergy; and the only time it was ever, in any form, laid before the Lower House of the Northern Synod (see *infra*, p. 121); and these were the limitations with which the reception was accompanied.

If there were any contrariety between what was done by the Convocations of 1604 and 1605, and by that of 1661, and it were necessary to consider to which the greater authority should be assigned, it is clear that the former were a much more full and complete representation of the clergy than the latter. The canons of 1604 and 1605, were the result of full deliberation by the Convocation of both provinces, untrammelled by any interference, actual or apprehended, on the part of the lay Parliament.

In 1661, the Convocation was dealing with a Prayer-Book originally sanctioned only by an Act of Parliament still prefixed to the book. The Southern Convocation was preparing a revision, which had to pass through the ordeal of parliamentary discussion, with a view to its being annexed to, and forming a schedule to, another Act of Parliament. The revision never really came before the Northern Convocation, as such, at all. This was owing to the matter being mixed up with parliamentary proceedings.

In June, 1661,[1] the House of Commons had appointed a committee—

(*a*) "To view the several laws for confirming the liturgy of the Church of England;

(*b*) "To make search whether the original book annexed to the Act passed in the fifth and sixth years of the reign of King Edward VI. be yet extant."

This shows that they were disposed to prefer the second book of Edward VI. to the first.

A Bill for Uniformity of Public Prayers and Administration of Sacraments was prepared, and, after passing all the stages in the Commons, was read a third time and sent up to the Lords

---

[1] Parker, Introduction, p. 84.

on July 9. But as the *original* book annexed to the Act 5 & 6 Edward VI. could not be found, a printed copy of James I.'s book, dated 1604, was annexed to the Bill, instead.

Here the matter was suspended. The Savoy Conference was then sitting. Parliament was adjourned on July 30, and did not meet again till November 30. Meanwhile (says Clarendon),[1] "The Bishops had spent the vacation in making such alterations in the Book of Common Prayer as they *thought would make it more grateful to the dissenting brethren*, for so the schismatical party called themselves; *and such additions as in their judgments, the temper of the present time, and the past miscarriages required*. It was necessarily to be presented to the Convocation, which is the national Synod of the Church; and that did not sit during the recess of the Parliament, and so came not together till the end of November.'

It seems probable that the alterations in the book made by the Bishops during the vacation, were embodied in "Cosin's Corrected Copy."

Lord Selborne[2] reasonably observes on this point: "The scheme of alterations, in the preparation of which the Bishops (some, probably, of those who had been Savoy Commissioners) spent this considerable interval of nearly four months, must of course have been written in a book, which book must afterwards have become the text on which the first deliberations of the Upper House proceeded. It must necessarily have expressed, not the views of any one mind, but their collective work; and if it was settled at meetings of Bishops only, no hand would be

[1] Life, vol. ii. p. 118.   [2] Notes, p. 44.

more likely to be employed than Cosin's. The book, which Mr. Parker calls Cosin's was, before its alteration by Sancroft, exactly such a record as must have been made of such a work—it extended even to the necessary directions for printing."[1]

He, therefore, concludes[2] "that (although some entries may have been made in it by Cosin long before) it was made up and assumed the character which alone gives it importance during the interval between the close of the Savoy Conference and the meeting of Convocation on the 21st of November in that year; and that it then represented the mind, not of Cosin only, but of others who were his fellow-labourers in the work."

Mr. Parker[3] disputes this conclusion, on the ground that he saw in the British Museum a letter "proving that Cosin returned to London" (after the vacation) on October 31. But he does not tell us when Cosin left London after the Savoy Conference; or show the impossibility of what is very probable, viz. that, the Bishops, having strongly upon their minds the urgent question of revision, might remain in consultation, after the breaking up of the Savoy Conference, *before* they went into the country; and that *then*, as well as during the three weeks which he himself shows that Cosin was in town before Convocation met, he might make the later entries in his corrected book, as the result of consultation with his brother Bishops.

That some such previous consultation had taken place, and that a very complete draft of a book—to be laid before Con-

---

[1] Parker, Introduction, pp. 94, 387, 388.
[2] Notes, p. 45.
[3] "Letter to Lord Selborne," p. 111.

vocation itself, or the committee, which could not be formally constituted till the King's letter of license had been formally read on the reassembling of Convocation—had been framed, is evident from the extraordinary rapidity with which it was then deemed necessary to proceed. Such rapidity would have been impossible, unless a complete understanding had been come to among the Bishops; not only as to the general principles, but as to the exact details of the revision; which could only have been done by previous consultation, and agreement on a basis laid down in *some such* form as "Cosin's Corrected Copy."

The motive for haste, was probably fear lest the Bill with the book of 1604 annexed, which had already been passed by the House of Commons, might be proceeded with in the Lords, without waiting for revision. Certainly the Convocation of Canterbury lost no time. On the first day of meeting, the royal letter authorizing it to revise the book was read, and a committee of eight Bishops appointed, to whom the Archbishop[1] *cum unanimi consensu confratrum suorum commisit vices suas . . . ad procedendum in dicto negotio.* They were to meet at the Bishop of Ely's house at five p.m. each day; and it is clear that the remaining work of the revision, must have been really done by them. On the following day, November 22, in two hours' of a morning sitting of the Upper House,[2] it got through the "Prefatory matter (except the *new* Preface), Kalendar, and Morning and Evening Prayer and Litany." This must have included the Ornaments Rubric, if (which there seems no reason

[1] Gibson, Synodus, p. 215.   [2] Parker, Introduction, 409.

to doubt) it was taken in its place. How much time could be given to this, which is now regarded by many as an *articulus stantis vel cadentis ecclesiæ*, may be inferred from a table printed by Mr. Parker,[1] drawn from comparison of the journals of the House, with the corrections actually made in the Convocation book." By this it appears that the two hours' work of that morning sitting involved, " 72 pages read, 1020 words erased, 2050 words added, 7 pages erased, and 3 pages added." In two hours more of an afternoon sitting, the same day was made, " Further progress, *say* the Collects, Epistles and Gospels," involving 155 pages read, 680 words erased, 1510 words added, 8 pages erased, 2 pages added.

The Ornaments Rubric must certainly have been passed by the Upper House, in the four busy hours of that day; for the first act on the following morning, November 23, was " Delivered the first part to the Lower House."[2]

On this same day, November 23, the Archbishop of York transmitted to "Mr. George Aislabie, at the Registrar's office, in the Minster Yard, York," three documents, which are printed " out of the Convocation book" at York, in Wake's "State of the Church," Appendix No. 158. These are so important for the light they throw on the impossibility of synodical acceptance of the Ornaments Rubric, as it now stands in the Prayer-Book, by the Clergy of the Northern Province, that, lengthy as they are, I transcribe the greater part of them.

1. A letter from the King to the Archbishop, "given at Whitehall, Nov. 22, 1661," in which, after reciting that he had,

[1] Introduction, p. 409.   [2] Synodus Anglicana, p. 215.

"on the 10th of June last," given the usual general "Royal License to treat," etc., to the Northern Convocation, his Majesty proceeds,[1] "We do hereby authorize and require that you review, or cause a review to be had and taken both of the Book of Common Prayer and of the ordinal; And after *mature consideration*, that you make such additions or alterations in the said books respectively as to you shall seem meet and convenient. Which our pleasure is, that you exhibit and present unto us in writing for our further consideration, etc."

2. Enclosing this royal letter, "By his majesties command," is another, addressed "to the Right Worshipful Dr. John Neile Prolocutor and the rest of his Brethren of our Convocation" as follows:—

"SIR,

"You see the contents of his majesty's Letters for the Review of the Book of Common Prayer and ordination etc for the despatch whereof his *Majesty requires all possible expedition*. His Grace and ourselves sit in consultation with the Bishops of the Province of Canterbury. And because the *time allotted for the despatch of these things is so short, and an Act of Parliament ready to passe, the ordinary course of concluding them here first*, then sending them down for your concurrence, and returning them up again, *is so dilatory, that it will not be consistent with his majesty's expectation*. It is therefore our desires and request to you, that forthewith you would passe a vote for a proxie in behalf of your whole house (wherein our

[1] The italics in this copy are mine, the capitals as printed by Wake.

Prolocutors are desired to concur) to Dr. Henry Fearne, Prolocutor, Dr. John Earles, Dean of Westminster, Dr. John Barwick Dean of Pauls, or to some other of the Lower House of Convocation there *conjunctim* and *Divisim*, to give your consent to such things as *shall be concluded* here in relation to the premisses. This Proxie under your Dean and Chapter and your Chancellours Seale we earnestly desire may (if possible) be sent up *by the next post* after this comes to your hands. This is all we have at present: We therefore commit you to the protection of Almighty God, resting

Your most affectionate friends,

" ACCEPT. EBOR.
JO. DURESME.
RICH. CARLIAL.
BRI. CESTRIANS."

3. Enclosing the two former was the following :—

" SIR,

" The enclosed to Doctor Neile your Prolocutor goes to him from All the Bishops of the Province, having in it a true copie of another from his majesty to myself. Deliver it I pray you unto him presently (excusing my not writing to him at present in particular) and *hasten their despatch* back according to the direction with as much speed as possibly you can; for it is of Great and General concernment. The Chancellor who hath been our clerk herein, will perhaps, (if at leisure) say more, I adding only this here in the close, that if *we have not*

All from you by the end of the next week we are lost. And in case the Convocation sit not, wish the Doctor presently to open the Letter as if it had been sent to himselfe only.

Farewell,
Yours,
ACCEPT. EBOR."

November 23.

"For Mr. George Aislabie, at the Register's office, in the Minster-Yard York."

November 23, 1661, was on a Saturday.

On the receipt of such missives from the Throne itself, and from the Metropolitan and all the Bishops of the province, Mr. Register Aislabie no doubt put his best leg foremost across the Minster-Yard, and by his efforts, the Dean, the Prolocutor, and Antony Elcock, S. T. P. the Archbishop's Commissary, were convened in the Chapter House. There, in præsentia mei Georgii Aislabie Notarii, in usual form the Dean præconized all persons who ought to have been there, "*diutius que expectatos*" (I wonder how long that day), and "*nullo mode comparentes, pronuntiavit contumaces.*" Then the King's and the Archbishop and Bishop's letters, as above, were read, and then "Iiden venerabiles viri unanimibus consensu et assensu suis cæterisque Personis tunc interessent: commissionem sive Procuratorium speciale fieri decreverunt et concedi" to the Prolocutor of the Southern Convocation and the two Deans named in the Bishops' letter, and of the Northern, to Henry Bridgeman, Dean of Chester; Robert Hitch, Prebendary of Holme in York Cathedral; and Matthew Smalwood, Proctor for the Archdeaconry of

Richmond; Andrew Sandiland, Proctor for the East Riding; and Humphrey Lloyd, Prebendary of Ampleford in York Minister.

The Procuratorium begins: "Nos Johannes Neile, S. T. P. Referendarius sive Prolocuter domus inferioris Sacræ Synodi sive Convocationis infra Provinciam Ebor, tentæ et celebratæ, nec non *cæteri Prælati et Clerici* in eadem congregati" (viz. the Dean and the Archbishop's Commissary) "*unanimibus nostris* Assensu pariter et consensu, venerabiles viros"—as above named, ordinamus, etc.—" nostros indubitatos Procuratores, etc., Damusque . . . eisdem Procuratoribus Nostris et eorum euilibet, potestatem generalem et mandatum speciale pro nobis, et vice, loco et nomine nostris, omnibus et singulis quæ in Sacra Synodo, sive Convocatione cleri Provinciæ Cant : jam apud Westmr : tent et celebrat ex Consilio et Deliberatione Communi, in negotio Revisionis *Libri Publicarum Precum, nec non formæ Consecrandi et Ordinandi,* etc. . . . Statui vel decerni contingerint consentiendi, et consensum et Assensum respective suos dandi et præbendi, aliisque ex adverso (si et quatenus, videbitur expediens dissentiendi et contradicendi ; et generaliter omnia et singuli alia faciendi, exercendi, et expediendi quæ in præmissis aut circa ea, necessaria fuerint seu Quomodolibet opportuna, etiamsi mandatum de se exigant magis speciale quam in præsentibus est expressum ; et quæ nosmet ipsi facere possemus si præsentes personaliter interessemus (Juribus, Libertatibus, *præminentiis* et consuetudinibus provinciæ et Ecclesiæ Eboracensis *dignitate et honore,* in omnibus semper salvis et *reservatis*); *Promittimus que* Nos Ratum Gratum et

Firmum *perpetuo habituros totum et quicquid dicti Procuratores nostri fecerint, vel eorum aliquis fecerit* in præmissis, *sub Hypotheca* et *obligatione* omnium et *Singulorum Bonorum nostrorum* et in ea parte cautionem *exponimus per præsentes.* In cujus rei testimonium sigillum Capitulare Ecclesiæ cath et metropoliticæ B. Petri prædict præsentibus apponi fecimus in domo Capitulari dictæ Ecclesiæ Ebor ultimo die Novembris. A.D. 1661."

These remarkable documents show—

1. That the Prayer-Book with the Ornaments Rubric as it now stands, was never, before it had become irrevocably fixed there, laid in any way before the Lower House at York representing the whole priesthood of the northern province.

2. That the synodical act, viz. the giving the Procuratorium above written, by which they were to be bound to receive the Rubric as a matter of "canonical obedience," was completed before the Synod itself could have any knowledge of the form it would assume.

3. That the Procuratores whom the Synod thus invested with all its own power and authority in *negotio revisionis, could* hold no consultation with the Synod which had thus created them its plenipotentiaries; for they were all contumaciously absent when the procuratorium was given; and must have started immediately, in order to be in time to execute the subscription in London at from eight to ten A.M. on the 20th of December.

The Archbishop's letter seems to have taken a week to reach York by post. The Procuratores must needs have taken longer time to prepare for, and execute the journey to London.

On the same November 23 on which the Archbishop's letter was despatched, the President of the Canterbury Convocation[1] sent for the Prolocutor and "tradidit ei *partem* libri publicarum *precum per hujusmodi domum examinat et revis,*" and directed that the Lower House "dictam partem cum omni celeritate qua potuit revideat, etc. This must have included the Ornaments Rubric as revised by the Upper House.

On the following Wednesday, November 27, the Prolocutor[2] retrodedit (the same) *partem libri* publicarum precum per *domum inferiorem examinat et revis una cum notula sive schedula emendationum sive* alterationum per eos fact,[3] "quam notulam sive schedulam obtulit domino præsidenti pro ejus et confratrum suorum consideratione et consultatione, etc. Deinde acceptata dicta notula sive schedula, per dictum præsidentem, dictus præsidens *dedit in manibus dicti prolocutoris residuam partem libri publicarum precum.* Eo que dismisso" proceeded to read the Schedulam, which was first *revis et examinat;* and then the Upper House proceeded to read through the Psalter, which with the Ordinal, formed another part with separate title in the book of 1636, used by Convocation, as the facsimile shows. The Ornaments Rubric must, therefore, have passed both Houses of the Canterbury Convocation before the procuratorium, binding the northern priesthood to accept it, was given at York; but

---

[1] Gibson, Synodus Anglicana, p. 215.   [2] Ibid. p. 216.
[3] Query: was this the list of alterations which is found in the MS. Convocation Book, see above, p. 91?

none of the clergy, in or out of that Synod, could possibly then know what form it had taken. If so, the York Procuratores, when they arrived in London, could have no effective consultation with the Synod there, on a matter already decided by both Houses. If any of them happened to be already in town, they could not even know the "honour thrust upon them," till the procuratorium arrived there. No doubt the Prolocutor of the Canterbury Synod, Dean Fern, must have been there, and have taken part in the discussions; and the same was probably true of the Deans of St. Paul's and Westminster, Barwick, and Earles. But the part taken by them was, in their real character as members of the Canterbury Synod, not in the fictitious character imposed upon them, when they were made to subscribe themselves as members of the Lower House at York.

Under these circumstances it is not surprising to find that the *form* of subscription, occupied what seems a very disproportionate amount of the time given to the revision, in the Upper House of the Canterbury Synod.

The original records in the Synodus Anglicana[1] show that the Upper House completed its revision of the whole book, except the Psalms, in which no alterations were made, the occasional prayers, and the ordinal, in *twelve* hours; viz. from eight to ten A.M., and from two to four P.M. on the first day; and from eight to ten A.M. on each the four following days to November 26. This involved, according to Mr. Parker's table, 302 pages read, 3840 words erased, 7920 words added, 18 pages erased, and 7 pages added.

[1] Gibson, Synodus Anglicana, pp. 215, 217.

On December 13, a committee was appointed from both Houses[1] "pro diligenti examinatione et revisione libri publicarum precum et administrationis sacramentorum, aliorumque rituum ecclesiæ Anglicanæ, *debita* forma *script exarat et.*"

This was apparently to superintend the "fairly copying out" of the manuscript book to be subscribed and annexed to the Act for Uniformity.

On all the days on which the Upper House sat at all, between November 22 and December 18, it only sat from eight to ten A.M. each day; but on December 19, it sat two hours both morning and afternoon, and the whole time was occupied in discussing the form of subscription;[2] which, after all, was settled by two Bishops, and the Vicars-General of London and Durham, at the Registry office.

At eight o'clock the following morning, December 20, time had been found after all the corrections (except a few, which appear to have been made after the subscription), to "fairly copy out" from the Convocation book, the whole matter, printed and MS. thereof, in the manuscript copy to be "annexed" to the Act for Uniformity; and from which the sealed books, to be "preserved in safety for ever in every Cathedral and Collegiate Church" (13 & 14 Car. II., sect. 28), were printed. At the end of this MS. book, either then or since the previous evening, were written four forms of subscription for the Upper and Lower Houses of the two Convocations, and subscribed respectively by the members then present from each.

[1] Gibson, Synodus Anglicana, p. 213.   [2] Ibid., p. 220.

The last of these, that for the Lower House of York, is, under the circumstances, so curious a document, that I transcribe it as it is printed by Mr. Parker[1]:—

"Nos etiam *universus clerus* inferioris Domus ejusdem Provinciæ Ebor *Synodice congregati* per n̄tros respective Procuratores sufficienter constitut: et substitut: dicto Libro Publicarum Precum, Administrationis Sacramentorum, et cum forma et modo ordinandi et Consecrandi, Episcopos, Presbyteros et Diaconos unanimiter concensimus et subscripsimus die et Anno prædictis.

"Henr. Fern, Matt. Smalwood,
"Jo. Barwick, Humfredus Lloyd,
"Rob. Hitch, And. Sundland."

Here, then, the unanimous consent of the *Universus Clerus* of the Lower House of the York Convocation, *Synodice congregati*, and through them, that of all the clergy of that Province, is supposed to have been given by the subscription of three of their number, to a Prayer-Book which none of the rest had ever seen; and by the further subscription of three other Procuratores, who did not belong either to that Convocation, or to the Province, none of the six having held any consultation on the subject, with the body, in or out of Synod, which they represented.

The subscription of the Procuratores could carry no greater authority than was inherent in those by whom the procuratorium was given. These, we have seen (p. 119), were the Prolocutor

[1] Introduction, p. 448.

and the Dean of York, and the Archbishop's Commissary, *Synodice congregati*,—with no previous notice given to themselves; and no notice at all to those whom they, then and there, pronounced contumacious for non-appearance,—to send the procuratorium *by return of post*.

I am no canonist. I have long been in perplexity and wonder what the phrase "canonical obedience," as now so frequently used, can mean. A comparison of this common use with co-existent facts, seems to interpret the phrase as signifying obedience to the rule which most commends itself to the conscience and taste of each individual clergyman. However that may be, I find it hard to believe that canon law can be so far removed from common-sense, that what took place in the Chapter House at York, on the last day of October, 1661, and the subscription at Westminster, on the 20th of December following, could, *as a matter of "canonical obedience,"* so bind the *Universus Clerius* of the province of York to a rubric which, as it stands, they had never seen, as to supersede the duty of obedience to the fifty-eighth canon of 1605.

Compare this hot haste in the Canterbury Convocation, and this fictitious representation, and impossibility of consultation, on the part of that of the Northern Province, with the deliberate and complete method, in which the canons of 1604 and 1605 were received by the "Church of England by full representation."

Though James I., with his notions of the royal prerogative, *circa sacra*, took upon him to promulge the canons of 1604 as "*per*[1] *utramque provinciam tam Cantuariensem quam Ebora-*

[1] Wilkins, vol. iv. p. 380.

censem diligenter observandi, when they had only been passed by the Canterbury Convocation; yet we find that, in its next session, March 17, 1605, the York [1] Convocation had claimed to have its voice heard; and obtained his royal license [2] to "treat, debate, consider, and consult of such canons, orders, etc. . . . as they should think necessary;" and, that then, reciting that they had "diligently viewed and deliberately examined the constitutions and canons ecclesiastical and every of them, concluded and agreed upon . . . by the Convocation of the province of Canterbury, they did decree and ordain that all and singular the said constitutions and canons ecclesiastical . . . be for ever hereafter of full power, force, and authority within the province of York, and be accounted and numbered among the constitutions and canons of the province of York." Can we doubt whether the reception of these canons, or that of the Ornaments Rubric, had, most fully, the authority of "the Church of England by representation"?

It is extraordinary how much these canons are ignored by those who take their stand upon the Ornaments Rubric, and yet are continually speaking of "canonical obedience;" while they set at nought the clear and explicit directions of the fifty-eighth canon, thus fully and deliberately passed by both Convocations.

We have now been sadly contemplating, for more than a year and a half, the melancholy spectacle of a highly conscientious clergyman choosing to remain in prison, and to be separated, finally, from a flock much attached to him, rather

---

[1] Wilkins, vol. iv. p. 426.   [2] Ibid., p. 428.

than promise to conform to *the fifty-eighth canon;* on the ground, as far as I can understand, that he feels his conscience rather bound by the proviso of an Act of Parliament, professedly based on the authority of another Act of Parliament; which, as it stands in the Prayer-Book, was never laid before the Synod of the province to which he belonged; and never, in the sense which he put upon it, obeyed, or in any way, (except by three proxies appointed by return of post,) accepted by the clergy of that province, for two hundred years. It seems to me that he was not bound by that proviso, as a matter of "canonical obedience;" but *only* by Act of Parliament. I understand that he refused to apply for his discharge from prison, on the ground that Lord Penzance was appointed by the two Archbishops under an Act of Parliament. Yet, as we have seen (p. 97), the Act, by the authority of which the ornaments were in the Church in the second year of Edward VI., treated the authority of "Archbishops, Bishops, and their Chancellors, Commissaries, Archdeacons, and other ordinaries, to inquire in their visitations, Synods, etc. . . . and to punish by *admonition, excommunication,* sequestration, or deprivation," cases of nonconformity to the Prayer-Book, as *given* to them "by virtue of that Act." It also gave full power to the secular *criminal* courts "to inquire, hear, and determine all manner of offences," *e.g.* "if any minister should use any other rite, ceremony, order, form, or manner of mass . . . than was mentioned and set forth in the said Book, as they might do against any person being indicted before them of trespass," *i.e.* by verdict of twelve forty shilling freeholders, directed by a judge at the assizes, and the Bishop, if it were his "pleasure," to occupy a seat on the bench ; or by the mayor of a borough, "to which the judges did not, then, commonly repair."

By the existing Act of Uniformity, 13 & 14 Car. II. c. 4, sect. 24, the laws and statutes then in force for uniformity, including the provisions for trial, are to "stand in full force" . . . with reference to the present Prayer-Book, and to "be applied, practised, and put in use for the punishment of all offences contrary to the said laws with relation to the Book aforesaid and no other." Mr. Green was therefore standing, in opposition to a plain canon of the Church, *on a proviso of an Act of Parliament*, based on a previous, and confirmed by a subsequent Act ; all three Acts giving power to purely secular courts to try clergymen as if they were trespassers ; and, in certain cases, to deprive and imprison them for life, for deviations from the Prayer-Book ; while, at the same time, he utterly denied authority to an ecclesiastical judge appointed by two Archbishops.

With profound respect for Mr. Green's conscientious self-sacrifice, I cannot but regard the position assumed by him, and his supporters, as full of inconsistencies, and confusion of ideas.

Mr. Green was no doubt bound, as every beneficed clergyman is bound, by the declaration, made in the church, when "reading himself in"—of "his unfeigned assent and consent to all and everything contained and prescribed in and by the Book of Common Prayer," etc. The necessity for making that declaration is imposed by the Act of Parliament, 14 Car. II. c. 4, sect. 3. The exact form of words in which it is to be made is prescribed therein.[1]

It seems to me that the principle on which the jurisdiction of Lord Penzance, and of the Judicial Committee, is altogether repudiated, would prevent a clergyman who holds it, from making that statutable declaration, or even require him to repudiate it, if already made.

That principle seems to me to involve the same confusion between "the things which are God's" and "the things which are Cæsar's," as that which He, who declared, to Cæsar's representative, that His "kingdom is not of this world," albeit the world was made by Him, at once exposed, and rebuked, in the case of the Pharisees.

A benefice, called spiritual because held in respect of a spiritual office, is, as consisting of things material, necessarily subject to Cæsar's jurisdiction. So is the exclusive right to minister in a certain building, which—though as spiritually dedicated to the service of God it is called a church—is yet, as material attached to the soil of the country, necessarily subject to the jurisdiction of the civil ruler of the country.

The courts called ecclesiastical, have often before them, extremely complicated and difficult questions, involving rights to such material things claimed in virtue of spiritual offices. This is so in almost all cases in which beneficed clergy, or even clergymen claiming to be beneficed (as was the case with Mr. Gorham, and as was threatened in that of Mr. Green), are concerned. In these cases, the jurisdiction which supports

[1] Ibid., § 4.

or disallows the claim to things *material as such*, must, *pro tanto*, be derived from the civil power. This is so, whether the Church is said to be "established" or not: as is not unfrequently seen in the case of dissenting chapels; and was recently seen in the case of the Bishop of Grahamstown *v.* the self-styled "dean" Williams.

The infelicitous phrase "established Church," is used to express the state of things,[1] in which,—besides, but not superseding, the ordinary law of the country as to property,—a special compact has been entered into between the civil power and the clergy, whereby property and material prerogative can be claimed by the latter, in respect of spiritual offices, on certain formulated conditions. To claim as Mr. Green and the President of the English Church Union, in the address which you sent me, claim—that the formulæ in which these conditions are expressed shall be interpreted only by persons holding spiritual offices—is to claim that the terms of a contract shall be interpreted only by, or on behalf of, the contracting parties on *one side*. A claim so unreasonable cannot possibly be maintained.

Every clergyman, on taking possession of the temporalities of a benefice, enters into a compact *with the civil power*, that he will hold them subject to the conditions laid down *in the Act for Uniformity*. The civil power must, by its *raison d'etre*, as controller of all things material within its jurisdiction, reserve the right to inquire whether the conditions of the compact, are fulfilled. So far as may be necessary for that purpose, it must claim the right to *interpret* the formularies of the Church

[1] See Letter by the Rev. T. T. Carter, Appendix III.

—not as matters of divine truth or human error, which is beyond its jurisdiction, but—as legal documents formulating the terms of the compact.

No doubt, questions have frequently arisen, and—while the kingdom which "is not *of* this world" continues to be *in* this world—must be expected to arise, in which the rulers of the lower kingdom, come into conflict with what really belongs to the law of the higher kingdom. In such cases, where the distinction is clear, there can be no doubt as to which is to be obeyed, in case the two conflict. But surely the King of kings, by His rebuke to the Pharisees, warns His servants to be careful not to confound the two, and, in a misguided zeal for God, claim for Him, the things which are Cæsar's. It seems to me such a confusion to claim the Ornaments Rubric as one of "the things which are God's." It originated in, and has been maintained by, successive Acts of Parliament, and bears its history on the face of it, as plainly as did Cæsar's tribute money.

In the sense put upon it by Mr. Green and his supporters, it was never obeyed by a parish priest, for three hundred years. The Clergy of the Northern Province were never consulted upon it, and over them its authority is solely derived from Acts of Parliament. Its only claim to the authority of the Church, arises out of what was done in the Canterbury Convocation of 1661. The procuratorium, sent by return of post from three clergymen at York,—convened at a moment's notice, with *no notice* given to any others,—is too flimsy a pretext to carry the slightest authority as a synodical act of the Northern Convocation.

We have seen the sense in which the Canterbury Convocation accepted the Rubric as altered, indicated by the nature of the verbal alterations made by the Revisers.

I submit that this sense is further made clear—1, by the public declaration of the leading Revisers, shortly before the meeting of that Convocation; 2, by other action in that Convocation itself; 3, by the general action of its members after it broke up. That the real motive of the Revisers and Convocation of 1661, for replacing Elizabeth's Rubric by the proviso of her Act, was, to maintain the use of the surplice by parliamentary authority, which might have been deemed wanting to it, if the Rubric had been altogether expunged; while, at the same time, they avoided the contest and excitement which would certainly have been stirred up if they had attempted to obtain the direct authority of Parliament for it, *eo nomine*, in any new form—that this was their real motive appears,—

1. From what was done by the leading Revisers in the vacation before the reassembling of the Convocation. The revision had been initiated by Charles II.'s warrant for the conference at the Savoy, of the preceding 25th of March,[1] addressed to twelve Bishops and certain orthodox divines, and to an equal number of the Presbyterian persuasion. In this he recites that, by his previous declaration of October 25,[2] he "did declare that he would appoint an equal number of learned divines of both persuasions to review the same (Book of Common Prayer) and to make such alterations therein as should be thought most necessary." Thereupon he did require and authorize them to meet at the Savoy, "to advise and consult

---

[1] Cardwell, Conferences, p. 257.   [2] Ibid., p. 299.

about the same; and, if occasion be, to make such reasonable and necessary alterations therein as by them might be agreed upon." They met and, as might have been anticipated, found, after prolonged discussions, that it would have been as easy for pure water and oil to mix, as for the two parties to agree upon anything; and so, for any practical purpose, the thing came to an abortive end.

The only tangible result was an elaborate paper drawn up by the Presbyterian "ministers" of "exceptions against the Book of Common Prayer," and an equally elaborate "answer of the Bishops to the same."

Under the head of Ceremonies, numbered xviii., the first complaint of the Presbyterian ministers is—

"That public worship may not be celebrated by any minister that dare not wear a surplice."[1] Upon this, and other ceremonies, viz. the cross in baptism, and kneeling at the Lord's Supper,[2] they "earnestly entreat the right reverend fathers and brethren to whom these papers are delivered to join with them in importuning his most excellent Majesty that his most gracious indulgence as to these ceremonies granted in his royal declaration may be confirmed and continued to us and our posterities," etc.

The declaration referred to, was that of October 25, 1660,[3] in which the King had said—

"For the use of the surplice, we are contented that all men be left to their liberty to do as they shall think fit without suffering in the least degree for wearing or not wearing it, pro-

[1] Cardwell, Conferences, p. 310.   [2] Ibid., p. 312.   [3] Ibid., p. 296.

vided that this liberty do not extend to our own chapel."
(When the Presbyterians sent to the Hague [1] before the restoration, they had been bold enough to ask, "that the use of the surplice might be discontinued by his chaplains, because the sight of it would give great offence and scandal to the people.") The King further provided "that the liberty should not extend to cathedral and collegiate churches, or to any college in either of our universities." He thus maintained the twenty-third, twenty-fourth, and twenty-fifth canons of 1604 and 1605. The ministers added further particular "exceptions" in the form of marginal notes to the Prayer-Book. On Elizabeth's Rubric, as it then stood, the "exception" is,[2] "Forasmuch as this rubric seemeth to *bring back the cope, albe, and other vestments* forbidden by the Common Prayer-Book, 5 & 6 Edward VI., and so our reasons alleged against ceremonies under our eighteenth general exception, we desire it may be wholly left out."

On this the Bishops reply:[3] "For the reasons given in our answer to the eighteenth general, whither you refer us, we think it fit that the rubric continue as it is."

We turn to the Bishops' answer to the eighteenth general, and find on the point in question only:[4] "This in brief may here suffice for the surplice, that reason and experience teaches that decent ornaments and habits preserve reverence, and are held therefore necessary to the solemnity of royal acts, and acts of justice, and why not as well to the solemnity of religious worship? And *in particular no habit more suitable than white*

---

[1] Cardwell, Conferences, p. 246.
[2] Ibid., p. 314.
[3] Ibid., p. 351, § 2, rub. 2.
[4] Ibid., p. 350.

linen, which resembles purity and beauty, wherein angels have appeared (Revelation xv.), fit for those where the Scripture calls angels; and this habit was ancient. Chrys. Ho. 60 ad po Antioch."

The Bishops' reasons, therefore, for "thinking it fit that the rubric continue as it is," were twofold :—

(1) General, that "decent ornaments and habits preserve reverence."

(2) Particular, that there is, for "the solemnity of religious worship, *no habit more suitable* than white linen."

The ministers had assigned as their reason for "desiring" that the rubric might be "wholly left out," that "it *seemeth* to *bring back* the cope, albe, etc., and other vestments." They did not allege that it ever had, in fact, brought back the "albe, etc., and other vestments," except the surplice, and the cope in cathedrals, etc. The contrary was too notorious to leave any ground for such an allegation. The mention of the other vestments was evidently a mere pretext to cover their real object, which was to get rid of the surplice. Before the King's restoration they had demanded, as a condition for giving him their help, that the surplice should not be used even in his own chapel; and on the principle of asking more and taking less, they probably expected at least to get what the King, as a matter of policy, had promised, viz. that the use should be left open to the choice of each minister. This object would be practically gained if they could get the Rubric struck out, and with it the direct coercive parliamentary authority for the surplice.

It is clear that the Bishops were determined to bar the attainment of this object, by keeping up the parliamentary authority of the Rubric, and, therein, of the surplice. If they intended no more than this, they might well disregard the pretended fears about the "albe, etc., and other vestments," and confine, as they did, their answer to the real question at issue, viz. the compulsory use of the surplice.

But if, as is now alleged, they did intend to do that very thing which the ministers only pretended to fear; and to bring *back* the albes and vestments; or rather to bring *in* the use of new vestments of the same kind; it is impossible to say that they acted honestly, in passing that point over, *sub silentio.*

But further, *if* this was the Bishops' secret intention; *if* their real motive was, that they thought, as some now think, that "white linen" was *less* "suitable" for the most solemn act of religious worship, than the various colours and materials characteristic of the chasuble—if they thought this, while they publicly declared that to "preserve the solemnity of religious worship *no* habit *was more* suitable than white linen," the statement was, on their part, a simple falsehood. Surely it is more credible, that they had no such intention, than that their words should so belie their thoughts.

Of the twelve Bishops who sat at the Savoy, all who belonged to the southern province were, of course, members of the Upper House of the Canterbury Convocation. The northern Bishops began to sit with the southern on June 21,[1] and continued to do so through the revision of the Prayer-Book. Walton,

---

[1] Synodus Anglicana, p. 210.

Bishop of Chester, who was one of the twelve, died on November 29, so that he probably could take no part in the following session; but Frewen of York, Cosin of Durham, and Sterne of Carlisle, did so.

We have seen,[1] that the first act of the Convocation, when it met in November, was to appoint a committee of eight Bishops to meet at Ely House (probably in consideration of the Bishop's (Wren's) age and infirmity) and that it *commisit* vices *suas, eisdem vel eorum tribus ad minus ad procedendum* in dicto negotio, viz. revisione libri precum publicarum." Of these eight, six, viz. Cosin, Wren, Morley, Henchman, Warner, and Sanderson, had sat at the Savoy, and concurred in the statement of reasons for retaining the Ornaments Rubric.

That the real work of the revision must have been done by this committee is evident; for the twelve hours in which the Upper House went through it (see p. 124) must have barely sufficed to read, formally, through the book as it came, revised, from the committee. That they judged this formal reading necessary, is shown by the fact that they read through the Psalms,[2] though no alterations were made in them.

Another of the Savoy Bishops, Sheldon, though not a member of the Ely House Committee, must have exercised much influence in the revision; for, owing to Archbishop Juxon's age, he, as Bishop of London, generally presided over the Upper House; and not only that position, but his character made him a leader of men. Burnet[3] tells us, as to that Lower House,

[1] Synodus Anglicana, p. 215.   [2] Ibid., p. 217.
[3] History of his own Times, vol. i. p. 184.

that such care was taken in the choice of members of the Convocation that everything went among them as was directed by Sheldon and Morley."

We may therefore conclude that the views expressed by the answers of the Bishops at the Savoy at the end of July, mainly directed the revision in the following November.

The Bishops' answers contain the only authoritative *reason published* for the retention of the Ornaments Rubric.

It is true that Cosin had, many years before, noted—in his prayer-books, used as commonplace books—an argument for the parliamentary legality of the vestments and alb, founded on (pace Mr. Parker) a mistaken view of the legal formalities required by the proviso of the Act of Elizabeth, and of the facts as to the Advertisements. Cosin had probably noted this, with a view to his litigation with Peter Smart.

The argument itself was evidently derived from a very puritanical document, published in 1606, called a "Survey of the Book of Common Prayer," in which[1] the anonymous writer attempted to prove the fifty-eighth canon illegal, as being opposed (which, no doubt, it was) to Elizabeth's Rubric. In like manner other puritanical writers took advantage of the Rubric, to bring discredit and odium upon the Church. But Cosin *never published* these notes. They remained in manuscript[2] till some of them were printed by Hiches in his "Two Treatises on the Christian Priesthood," published in 1707; and the whole by Nicholls, in his "Commentary on the Common Prayer," published in 1712.

[1] Cosin, Works, vol. v. p. 42.   [2] Ibid., preface xiv.

They then, as Lord Selborne says,[1] "became the fountain-head of a new tradition, afterwards carried on by several writers of the eighteenth and present centuries—by Nicholls, S. Gibson, Wheatley, John Johnson, Burn, Cardwell, and others, reversing that of Hooker, Sparke, Lestrange, Wren, Heylyn, Sparrow, and every other *earlier* churchman of views similar to Cosin's, except Cosin himself." And I venture to add that, *except* in the solitude of his study, when forging a weapon wherewith to fight Peter Smart, there is no ground for regarding Cosin himself as *practically* an exception among the churchmen named by Lord Selborne, of whom Wren the Nestor of Ely House, Heylyn, and Sparrow, co-operated with him at the Savoy.

I have seen no evidence that Cosin ever followed out the argument of his notes into any overt act. We have seen (*supra*, p. 89) that he joined in the alteration of the Durham vestments as *not* being, till they were changed, "according to the canons and constitutions of the Church of England." In his visitation articles, as Archdeacon of the East Riding, 1627, he inquired in article fourteen[2] as to the minister: "Doth he in the time of public and divine service, as well morning and evening, and *at all other times of his ministration*, when *any Sacrament be administered*, or any other rite and ceremony of the Church solemnized, *use* and wear *the surplice* without any excuse or pretence whatsoever? And doth he never omit the same?"

In the manuscript draft of visitation articles, published by the Surtees Society,[3] this article runs, "Doth he not only

---

[1] Notes, 28.   [2] Works, vol. ii. p. 9.
[3] Cosin, Correspondence, vol. i. p. 113.

sometimes weare, or usually weare, but always weare and never omit the wearing of a surplice when he readeth Divine Service either morning or evening, or when he *administereth the Sacraments*, and performeth *any other part of his priestly* or ministerial function in the church?" He clearly considered the surplice to be the proper *priestly* vestment.

He clearly, then, thought, that for the habit of the minister "at all times of his ministration, when any Sacrament be administered," none was "more suitable than white linen," as he and the other Bishops said at the Savoy.

We have seen above (p. 113) that Lord Clarendon, who must have known much of the actions and intentions of the Bishops, tells us that "they spent the vacation in making such alterations in the Book of Common Prayer as *they thought would make it more grateful to the dissenting brethren*, for so the schismatical party called themselves." That some, at least, of the Bishops at the Savoy manifested this conciliatory disposition; and that of these, *quod minime reris*, Cosin was one; we are told by the leading spirit of the opposite camp, Richard Baxter. The active part he took in the matter, rendered him a very competent and, on the point before us, an unexceptionable witness.[1]

He gives some graphic notes as to the regularity of attendance, bearing, and character of the several Bishops at the Savoy. He confirms Burnet's statement, that Sheldon and Morley were the ruling spirits among them.

"The Bishop of London" (Sheldon), he says, "only appeared

[1] *Reliquiæ Banterianæ*, p. 363.

the first day ... but all men supposed that he and Bishop Morley, and, next, Bishop Henchman, were *the doers and disposers of all.* Bishop Cosin was there constantly, and had a great deal of talk, with so little logic, natural or artificial, that I perceived no one much moved by anything he said. But two virtues he had—one, he was excellently well versed in canons, councils, and fathers, which he remembered when, by citing any passage, we tried him; the other, he was of a rustick wit and carriage ... more affable and familiar than the rest.

"Bishop Gauden *was our constant helper.* He and Bishop Cosin seldom were absent. ... But when we got some *moderating concessions* from him and *Bishop Cosin* by his means, the rest came in and broke them off."

If,—while thus acting so as to lead Baxter to think him disposed to make concessions to the presbyterian party,—Cosin was secretly intending to bring about a revival of "albs and other vestments," so far from "grateful to the dissenting brethren;" he was acting a part, to characterize which, one would be tempted to use very strong language. *Credat* who can, *non ego.*

2. We come to other action of the same Convocation. On June 21, 1661, the day on which the northern Bishops began to sit with the southern,[1] the Bishop of London presiding, "cum confratribus suis tractatum habuit de conceptione unius libri *articulorum in visitatione cujuslibet episcopi* œconomis et inquisitoribus in qualibet diocesi ministrandorum."` They appointed, for that purpose, a committee of six southern

[1] Synodus Anglicana, p. 210.

Bishops, and invited three northern Bishops, viz. Durham, Carlisle, and Chester, "in dicto negotio esse interessentes et assistentes," with the former. What this committee did, does not appear; but on February 21 following,[1] we find "cura concipiendi articulos in visitationibus observandos, domino Johanni (Cosin) episcopo Dunelm commissa et relata;" and, on March 8, he,[2] "secundum mandatum ei datum, et curam ei commissam, introduxit et tradidit in manibus domini præsidentis *librum articulorum visitationem concernen.* alias per eum concept." which book was referred to the Archbishop of Canterbury, "pro ejus perlectione et debita consideratione eorundem et pro eorum emendatione, reformatione et correctione sua."

Mr. Parker,[3] quoting this, observes, "This passage probably refers to the articles of inquiry, etc." by Cosin, 1662, reprinted in Cosin's Works, vol. iv. p. 505. He continues, "Visitation articles, issued by *seventeen Bishops during the* year 1662, are extant, and *on comparison they are found very similar to those of Bishop Cosin.*"

Cosin's articles of 1662—prepared by him under such a special commission from the Convocation; sent for revision by the Archbishop of Canterbury; and issued by Cosin after he must have seen the alterations, if any, made by the Archbishop; and mainly adopted by seventeen Bishops in the same year—must fairly be taken to represent the mind of the Bishops who took part in that Convocation.

[1] Synodus Anglicana, p. 225. [2] Ibid., p. 226.
[3] Introduction, p. 463, note.

On the matter of ministerial apparel, the articles ask the churchwardens—[1]

6. Have you a *large and decent surplice* (one or more) for the minister to *wear at all times of his public ministration* in the Church?

And "concerning ministers, etc."[2]—

4. Doth he always at the reading or *celebrating any divine office*" (which surely must include Holy Communion) " constantly wear the surplice and other his ecclesiastical habit according to his degree? and doth he never omit it?"

These articles—considering the circumstances under which they were issued—amount to a contemporary exposition, showing the *animus imponentis*; put forth by authority of the Convocation itself, which gave the sanction of the Church to the Ornaments Rubric; and explanatory of the sense in which they understood the words "ornaments of the ministers *at all times of their ministrations.*"

We have seen (*supra*, p. 111) that the words italicised, were the only words added by the Revisers to those of the proviso in the Act of Elizabeth; and that they were taken from her Rubric, but with erasure of the words by which they were there preceded —" at the time of the Communion." That omission made all times of their ministrations homogeneous in respect of the ornaments of the ministers; and therefore excluded the ornaments specially appropriated by the first book of Edward VI. to the time of Holy Communion. The " *large* and decent surplice " required by Cosin's article, was evidently the *superpelliceum idque*

---

[1] Cosin, Works, vol. iv. p. 508.   [2] Ibid., p. 510.

manicatum of the fifty-eighth canon, and therefore incapable of being used *with* the Edwardian vestments (*supra*, p. 87).

When the country clergy of 1662, got their new Prayer-Books; and found these articles simultaneously issued by the Bishops, under sanction of the Convocation itself; how could they possibly imagine that the Convocation intended, that they should begin to use, for the celebration of Holy Communion,— *not* the " large surplice," which the articles said the minister was " to wear at all times of his ministration ;" but some other vestments, of which the author of the articles had written,[1] " they are so unknown to many, that by most they are neglected?" Yet no hint to help them, did his articles give.

It is easy to say they might find them mentioned in the first book of Edward VI., now that the matter has been much discussed, and the old Prayer-Books reprinted. But in 1662, the case was very different. The first book of Edward VI. was then so rare, that it is doubtful whether Cosin himself knew it in the original vernacular. The editor of his works for the Anglo-Catholic Library, vol. v. preface xix., observes, " that when Cosin wrote what forms a part of them " (the Third Series of Notes), " namely, the reference to the First Book of Common Prayer, 2 Edward VI., and to Bucer's exceptions to it, *he used not that Prayer-Book*, but the Latin translation, by Alesius, reprinted in Bucer's " Scripta Anglicana," *in consequence of which many erroneous statements have been made by him.*" How, then, were the " country parsons " of 1662, to be acquainted with the book, " having no man to guide them ;" and not a word said in

---
[1] Cosin, Works, vol. v. p. 507.

the visitation articles, except in implied opposition to special vestments for "the time of the Communion?"

The preamble of sect. 2 of the Act for Uniformity, enacting the use of the revised Prayer-Book, recites, "to the intent that every *person within this realm may certainly know the rule to which he is to conform* in Publique Worship and Administration of the Sacraments, etc. . . . be it enacted" that the book annexed be used. *If* the Convocation, which prepared the book annexed, intended that the Edwardian vestments should be used with it, they certainly took great care that *no man* should "certainly know the rule to which he was to conform." That a great legislative body of reasonable men, should enact a rule for all the clergy, including themselves; and keep the rule a profound secret,—again I say, *credat* who can, *non ego*.

3. What was done by the members of the revising Convocation afterwards? Well, the Bishops went on issuing the same visitation articles, as to the *large surplice* for the minister to wear "at all times of his public ministration in the church." In the appendix to the "Report of the Royal Commission on Ritual," p. 615, are given Bishop Morley's articles for the diocese of Winchester, 1661, in which the same question as to the surplice for all ministrations is asked as in Cosin's: and a note is added by the editor of the report, "Collated with copies of the following articles which *are all re-issues of the same text*." Then follow the names of *twenty* bishops, with the dates of their articles ranging from 1662 to 1683.

In 1686, Sancroft, then Archbishop of Canterbury, issued "Articles for the Diocese of Lincoln, in his Metropolitical

Visitation." These are printed in the appendix to the "Report of the Royal Commission on Ritual," p. 653, as collated with a copy of his articles for the diocese of Canterbury in 1682. In both is repeated the same question as to the "large surplice for all ministrations;" and, that "all ministrations" included Holy Communion, is, *ex abundanti*, made clear by article seven, "concerning the Clergy." "Doth your Parson, Vicar, etc., read Divine Service on all Sundays and Holy days; and publicly administer the Holy Sacraments of Baptism and *the Eucharist*, and perform all other ministerial offices and duties, in such *manner and form, as is directed by the Book of Common Prayer lately established*, and the Act of Uniformity therewith published, and the three offices before mentioned, without *addition, diminution, or alteration?* And doth he in these *his ministrations* wear the *Surplice*, with a Hood or Tippet befitting his degree?"

The mention of the hood, etc., shows that Sancroft held the fifty-eighth canon to be still in force; and the whole article shows, that "the manner and form directed by the Book of Common Prayer lately established," required the minister to wear the surplice when he "administered the Holy Sacrament . . . of the Eucharist;" and admitted on that and all other points, like the fourteenth canon, of no "addition, diminution, or alteration." Sancroft clearly no more dreamt than anybody else, till quite recently, of the surplice being merely permitted as a *minimum*; or of the vestments being intended at all.

But no one could be more intimately acquainted with the mind of the Revisers, and the Convocation of 1661, than he. He had written with his own hand,—probably, the whole of the alterations made at Ely House, and certainly the whole of the alterations as finally agreed to, in the Convocation itself—in the "Convocation Book," from which the "Annexed Book" subscribed by the members was fairly copied out; and which was, itself, laid before both Houses of Parliament.

So much for the contemporary exposition of the Ornaments Rubric by the Bishops who synodically enacted it. What was the contemporary practice under it?

If there were any places in England where we might expect to find the strictest conformity to the ritual of the Prayer-Book as recently revised, those places were Bishop Cosin's private chapels, at Durham and Auckland.

In the auditor's office at Durham, is preserved a deed executed by Cosin on July 11, 1667; within six years from the revision of the Prayer-Book;[1] by which he gives to his successors as Bishops of Durham, "vasa quædam argentea, dupliciter deaurata, una cum quibusdam libris, palliis, aliisque ornamentis, quæ in *schedulâ præsentibus additâ specificantur:* eo fine ut semper inservient et usurpentur ad divinarum celebrationem, tum in sacello nostro et successorum nostrorum quod nuper ereximus et consecravimus in Castro nostro Episcopali de Auckland, tum in capellâ quam nuperrime etiam instauravimus in Castro nostro Dunelmensi.

Cosin refers to this deed in his will,[2] where he mentions that he laid out a thousand pounds in furnishing these chapels.

[1] Surtees Society, Cosin Correspondence, vol. ii. p. 168.
[2] Ibid., p. 295.

The schedule referred to in the deed, condescends to such particulars as "duo *hypogonatica* (kneeling cushions), rubro panno cooperta et circumfimbriata, pro boreali et australi partibus Altaris."

Now, if Cosin, notwithstanding his public acts and utterances, was still entertaining an esoteric intention to bring about the use of the Edwardian vestments, as a kind of *Disciplina Arcani*, here was an excellent opportunity for him to show how it should be done. But in the full inventory in his *schedula*, including other *hypogonatica*, there is no mention of any such thing as alb or chasuble, but only of "*duodecim superpellicea*, quorum octo pro viris, quatuor reliqui pro organista, clerico sacelli, et pueris eidem servientibus," and two purple gowns—"*togæ melibei coloris*, quarum una pro organista, altera pro clerico sacelli."

But these are words and deeds from the *Upper* House of the Convocation of 1661. We lay-people have now been diligently taught—by the clergy who claim to be most catholic—that, though Bishops in the abstract, are a very sacred institution, yet Bishops in the concrete, *ont toujours tort*. We are not therefore surprised to be told of episcopal misbehaviour. How, then, about the clergy of the Lower House of Canterbury, in 1661? We know that the Lower House at York was never consulted about the Ornaments Rubric, as it now stands, at all. But if the Bishops of both provinces intended to revive the Edwardian vestments, surely the clergy of the Lower House of Canterbury must have been let into the secret; because they themselves, and those whom they represented, would be the persons who, most, would have to use the vestments. Was this ever done by any member of that Lower House?

In the "Hierurgia Anglicana" edited by members of the Cambridge Camden Society, including, I believe, the late Dr. Neale, is a collection of all the evidence the editors could find, as to elaborate ritual used with the English Prayer-Books. The editors (p. 173, note) contend that the fifty-eighth canon was superseded by the Rubric of 1661, and that the Edwardian vestments are still required; but, like other writers on that side, they give no evidence of the actual use of chasubles, etc., except the malicious and *false* statements of puritanical writers; *e.g.* "Hierurgia Anglicana," p. 111, they quote from the puritanical "Admonition to Parliament," 1572, the statement as to ordinations: "Now there is required a surplice, a *vestment*, a *pastoral staff*," etc. But they add, in a note, "Whitgift, however, calls this 'a false and untrue report'" ("Defence of the Answers").[1]

[1] It is remarkable that the keen scent of the authors of the "Admonition to Parliament," for "Popish baggage," and of the editors of the "Hierurgia Anglicana," for ornate ritual in the English Church, could, in allied quest, unearth no better evidence as to vestments than this scrap; instantly refuted by Whitgift's, "reade the book (the ordinal) from beginning to end." The "Admonition" itself, by what it says and does not say, proves that the vestments, chasuble and alb were, then, completely outside both law and practice. I have it as printed paragraph by paragraph alternately with his own answer, by Whitgift, in 1572. On p. 236, the admonishers complain that "copes, caps, surplesses, tippets, and suche like baggage, the preaching signes of Popish priesthood, the Popes creatures, kepte in the same forme to that ende, to bring dignitie and reverence to the ministers and sacraments, should be *reteined* still and not abolished." This is from the second part of the Admonition, entitled "A view of Popish abuses yet remayning in the English Church, for the which godlie ministers have refused to subscribe."

On page 148, they say of the "booke of common prayer for the Church of

They *did* refer to a statement, that there is in the church of Wensley, in Yorkshire, a brass, commemorating a Jacobean divine arranged in chasuble, etc. But Canon Raine[1] says: "The truth is, that Oswald Dyke, the rector of that church, who died in 1607, is buried under the tombstone of one of his predecessors. The brass is certainly not later in date than the earliest part of the fifteenth century. If this is not sufficient, I bring Mr. Dyke's will in evidence. He desires in it 'to be buried in the quier of Wenslow, under the stone where Sir Simon de Wenslow was buried, havinge this superscription, *non moriar sed vivam et narrabo* opera Domini.' This quotation occurs upon the stone, and I have shown elsewhere who Sir Simon de Wensley was."

As to the alb, the editors of the "Hierurgia Anglicana" say (p. 130, note), "The only instance of its being worn after the England authorized by Parliament: this booke is an imperfecte booke, culled and picked out of the Popish dunghill, the masse booke." That men taking this unamiable view of the "masse booke,"—supposing alb and chasuble, the special vestments of the mass, to be still *retained* in the English Church,—should not have included them with "copes, caps, surplesses, tippets, and such like baggage," is inconceivable. The inference, then, is to me irresistible, that alb and chasuble were not then included among the "ornaments of the second year of Edward VI. still to be *retained* and in use;" but that "other order had been taken," and the temporary proviso of the Act of 1 Elizabeth, c. 2, made no longer applicable to them.

This conclusion is further proved by what the admonishers speak of as the then existing law, p. 235 : "For the order of administration of sacraments and common prayer enough is sayde before ; *all the service* and *administration is tyed* to a *surplesse*, in *cathedral churches*, they must have *a cope*." This is clearly a summary of the "order" as to apparel, "taken" in the Advertisements.

[1] "Vestments in the Northern Province," p. 13, note.

Restoration, which we know of, was in 1660, at a consecration of Bishops in Dublin." They did, however, later (p. 167), find mention of albs being used at the enthronization of Bishop Walton in Chester Cathedral, in 1661. One can hardly help suspecting that these were really the other *vestes albæ*, viz. loose surplices, rather than close-fitting albs. The latter, used alone, would be rather suggestive of a very incomplete morning toilette.

Walton's republican preface to his great Polyglott Bible, was scarcely consistent with "ritualistic proclivities" on his part.

These instances, whatever they amount to, were previous to the Convocation of 1661. The statement of the "Hierurgia Anglicana" as to the latest use of albs, and its silence as to any use of chasubles after the close of that Convocation, is very strong evidence that those vestments were not used by the priests who had been members of the Lower House in it.

In your letter (p. 9) you say, of that Convocation, "The Church ... as it seems to me, most wisely raised the standard to its old height, and bade her children aim at it; while, like a tender mother, she refrained from forcing them up to it."

As to the "standard being raised to its old height," may I again ask your attention to the point referred to in my first letter (p. 4); viz. the fact that, while the Revisers erased from the Ornaments Rubric, the then existing reference to the time of the Communion; they deliberately reinstated—after having at first materially altered it[1]—the rubric immediately prefixed to the Communion, which directs that the table, at the communion-

[1] That alteration *was* included in Sancroft's MS. list of "material alterations."

time, having "a fair white linen cloth upon it, shall stand in the Body of the Church, or in the Chancel, where Morning and Evening Prayer are appointed to be said."[1] You will, I think, hardly deem *this* Rubric as belonging to the "old standard" of the second year of Edward VI., dating, as it does, from 1552.

What would be symbolized by a priest, in chasuble and alb, ministering at a table placed near the reading-desk, whether that were in the body of the church or in the chancel?

Is it likely that the same Convocation should have deliberately sanctioned ritual so inconsistent?

Can you explain why those who feel themselves so strictly bound by the Ornaments Rubric,—taken without any reference to its subsequent history,—do not feel themselves equally bound by the much plainer meaning of this Rubric standing in immediate connection with the office for Holy Communion, and adopted in place of an alteration directing that the table should stand in "the upper end of the chancel?"

If the clergy, in the Convocation of 1661, intended to make the use of chasuble and alb the rule of the English Church, it seems to me that, instead of being true representatives of the Church as a "tender mother," they were much more like those of whom it was said, "they bind heavy burdens ... and lay them on men's shoulders; but they themselves will not move them with one of their fingers."

Surely here, again, charity and common-sense lead us rather

---

[1] As something turns upon the punctuation, the commas in the above are placed as in the photozincographed facsimile of Sancroft's MS. restoration of the old rubric in the "Convocation Book."

to believe that they did *not* intend to impose on others, the "burdens which they themselves did not move with one of their fingers."

That large assemblies of practical Englishmen—first of Bishops and clergy in Convocation, and then of laymen in Parliament—legislating under a preamble which set forth their objects to be an "universal Agreement in the Publique Worship of Almighty God; and to the intent that *every person* within this Realm, may *certainly know* the *Rule to which he is to conform* in Publique Worship and Administration of Sacraments, and other Rites and Ceremonies of the Church," etc.; were intending to "raise a standard" to which some enlightened clergymen in an "ideal Church of the future," two centuries afterwards, might attain; but of which no Bishop, priest, or layman that then was, ever publicly expressed, in word or deed, the slightest notion—this is a view which transcends the limited range of my faculties to realize.

§ VII.—Primitive Sacerdotal Habit.

In my first letter (p. 5) I had spoken of the rejection of the vestments by (what I venture to think proved) a consensus of the whole English clergy, *semper, ubique, ab omnibus,* for three centuries. You ask, in reply, "But what do you say of the consensus of *clerus totus* for centuries much more than three?"

My inquiry having reference only to action under the Ornaments Rubric, I did not go further back; but I should be quite willing to go with you into the earlier centuries, if you are willing not to stop short in the Middle Ages. But anything like a full inquiry would make this letter—already far too long—utterly intolerable. I will but mention a few points. As to the chasuble, Dr. Rock, who, as a learned ritualist of the Roman obedience, was likely to be free from "insular prejudices," says, in his "Hierurgia," p. 439: "Up to the sixth century the pœnula was a *civic* habit, and worn without discrimination by laymen and ecclesiastics. From the pœnula," he says (p. 438), "is derived our chasuble."

During, then, those earlier centuries—the age of the great councils and Fathers, to which our Church continually appeals—the chasuble was not a distinctively sacerdotal, still less *the* specially eucharistic vestment. As such, it cannot, therefore, claim to be called catholic.

The late Mr. Wharton Marriott has gone much more fully into the matter, and filled his large octavo, the "Vestiarium Christianum," with a collection of ancient authorities, and figured illustrations on the subject. The use of different names, *pœnula*, *casula*, and *planeta*, for a garment essentially of the same kind, creates some difficulty in tracing the matter out; but there can be no doubt as to the general result. The planeta, or pœnula, seems to have been generally a garment more ornate, and of finer quality, used by the rich; and the casula coarser, for the poor, and for outdoor use.

Of this latter, an instance occurs in St. Augustine's "De Civitate Dei," lib. xxi. c. 8, sect. 9, where, among instances of the supernatural, or special providences, he relates how "erat quidam senex Florentius Hipponensis noster, homo religiosus et pauper; sartoris se arte pascebat, *casulam* perdiderat, et unde sibi emeret non habebat. Ad viginti Martyres quorum memoria apud nos est celeberrima, clara voce ut vestiretur oravit." He soon after found on the shore, a large fish, just thrown up, which he sold to an honest keeper of a cook-shop; who, finding inside it a gold ring, returned that to the poor tailor, saying *ecce quomodo viginti martyres te vestierunt.*

Of the ornate planeta, is figured on this page an illustration taken from the large work of Padre Garucci,[1] on the gilt glass

---

[1] Padre Garucci, in his work, "Vetri Ornati de Figure in Oro," concludes, from a learned inquiry, that these *vetri* were never, as some have supposed, used in celebrations of the Holy Eucharist—"che i vasi cimiteriali di vetro non furono mai destinati al sacrifizio dell altare; ne anche a communicare i fedeli,"—but for Christian family festivals, as indicated by the

vessels which have been found in the Roman catacombs. The specimen from which this figure was taken has been brought to England, "and thereby hangs a tale." It was exhibited at the Wolverhampton Church Congress, where Dr. Littledale said of it,[1] "In this glass is depicted a *priest, vested* in *just such a chasuble as may now be seen* in ritualistic churches." I myself saw the same specimen in an art collection at Leeds. There was clearly on it just such a figure, with hands uplifted, as in prayer, as Dr. Littledale described. But the glass, being somewhat mutilated, and in that part less distinct, it required closer examination to discern what was, though less clearly, there—a second figure standing by the side of the first; and this certainly that of a *lady*, in gay attire. An exactly similar figure appears on another vase of the same kind, figured in Mr. J. H. Parker's "Archæology of Rome," "The Catacombs," Vases, Plate vii. 2, and described by him as "a lady richly attired in the costume of the eighth or ninth century, wearing a cap, and with the hands uplifted in the oriental attitude of prayer."

Mr. Marriott's[2] conclusion from other details in this specimen, is that the figures "are man and wife, people of high rank; the scroll between them represents the *tabulæ matrimoniales*; the coin just below, the marriage dowry; the bishop's chair is

---

subjects, on the occasion of funerals, marriages, baptisms, "o di altre feste civile di cristine famiglie." (Prefazione xvi.) *E.g.* some, he says, as bearing representations of betrothed or wedded pairs, were made for nuptial festivals: "altri poi mi sembrano fatti per feste nuziali, essendovi rappresentati i due sposi o i due conjugi." Such seems the one before us.

[1] *Guardian*, Oct. 18, 1867, p. 1121, col. b.
[2] Vestiarium Christianum, p. 248.

suggestive of the Church, and more particularly of the cathedral church; and the tree, with its fruit, probably of the tree of life."

There is a superscription, "DIGNTIAS AMIC," which, he notes, is a mistake of the original workman for DIGNITAS AMIC. The full inscription for which these words stand representative, is "Dignitas Amicorum vivas cum tuis feliciter," which is found on other more complete specimens.

We have, then, here, Dr. Littledale's "just such a chasuble as may now be seen in ritualistic churches," worn, not by a priest, but by a Roman grandee, with his betrothed, or bride, in the height of the fashion of the eighth or ninth century. Clearly, by whatever name it might be called, it was not the specially sacerdotal vestment of the period.

Mr. Marriott[1] concludes, from his examination of the documents, that "there is no certain evidence of the word *casula* ever being employed in speaking of a vestment of Christian ministry before the ninth century of our era."

This being so, of the sixteen Christian centuries which preceded the date of the Ornaments Rubric, the chasuble cannot, at the utmost, claim a prescription of more than seven. Those seven centuries were, no doubt, the period during which, most, the Church, was

". . . . thronèd high,
And compassed with the world's too tempting blazonry."

But they were not, therefore—rather, therefore they were not—

[1] Vestiarium, p. lxiii.

the purest ages, or those most truly representative of the kingdom not of this world.

How far other they were, is seen in the ominous words with which one eminently free from "insular prejudice," Baronius, opens their history:[1] "En incipit annus Redemptoris nongentissimus quo et novum inchoatur sœculum, quod sui *asperitate, ac boni sterilitate, ferreum, malique exundantis deformitate, plumbeum, atque inopia scriptorum*, appellari consuevit *obscurum*. In ejus limine constituti, ob ea quæ pro foribus *adeo flagitiosa* nuper contigit aspexisse, antequam progrediamur ulterius, hic lectorem monendo præfari aliquid necessarium duximus, ne quid scandali pusillus animo patiatur, si quando videre contigerit *abominationem desolationis* in templo, sed magis miretur, et cognoscat in ejus custodia divinam invigilare potentiam, cum non ut olim, *abominationem tantam* secuta mox fuerit desolatio templi, intelligatque solidioribus illo niti hoc fundamentis, nempe promissionibus Christi."

Is the chasuble commended to us by the fact, that its first appearance as a sacerdotal vestment, synchronizes with this age of iron, of lead, of darkness, of abomination of desolation?

It is a relief to turn from the sickening thought of those evil times, to "earlier purer days," and inquire what was then the sacerdotal vestment.

Mr. Marriott's conclusion[2] from his elaborate inquiry,—which I have not seen seriously controverted, still less disproved,—is "that of all the various types of ministering dress now retained

---

[1] Baronii, Annales Ecclesiastici, tom. x. p. 629.
[2] Vestiarium, p. lxxxii.

in different branches of the Church, there is one, and one only, which approaches closely both in form and distinctive ornament to that of primitive Christendom, that dress being the surplice with scarf or stole now worn in the English Church." He adds in a note, " The only difference is that the black stripes represented on those primitive vestments *were attached to the tunic* instead of being separate, as was the later orarium and the modern stole."

This conclusion is made clear to the eye by plates appended to the " Vestiarium," taken from the catacombs, especially Plates xi., xii., xiv., xv., xvii., lxiii.

A similar conclusion has been arrived at by Mr. J. H. Parker.[1] He says, " The costume of the modern English Clergy is very nearly a copy of that of the *oranti* in the catacombs and the apostles, who are represented in the same costume." He adds in a note, " The apostles, introducing the saints to Christ, in the mosaic pictures in the churches, from the sixth to the ninth centuries, are represented in a costume closely resembling the surplice and stole." These observations are illustrated in Mr. Parker's work, especially by Plate xxiii., and those of the gilt vases iv. and vii.

These Anglican representations are entirely borne out by plates in De Rossi's " Roma Sotteranea Christiana," issued from the cromolitografia Pontificia, especially tom. ii., tavv. v., vii.,[2] xx.

[1] Archæology of Rome, Catacombs, p. 9. See also his work on the Mosaic Pictures of Rome, pp. 19, 20; plates ix., xii., xiii.
[2] See Frontispiece to this volume and Appendix I.

On the question of colour, Mr. Marriott says,[1] "On a review, then, of the whole evidence from early literature bearing upon this question, we should conclude, without doubt, that the dress appropriate to the most solemn offices of holy ministry, during the primitive age, was *white*."

Of many authorities given by him, I will only quote one, St. Jerome "Adversus Pelagianos," lib i. vol. ii. p. 177, where, rebuking the affected austerity of some of these, he says, " Repente mutaris in Stoicum et de Zenonis nobis tonas supercilio . . . unde adjungis gloriam vestium et ornamentorum Deo esse contrarium. Quæ sunt rogo, inimicitiæ contra Deum si tunicam habuero mundiorem: si Episcopus Presbyter et Diaconus, et reliquus ordo Ecclesiasticus, *in administratione sacrificiorum candida veste* processerint?"

From the æsthetic point of view, Dr. Rock,[2] writing in 1833, respecting his own communion, says, "It is much to be lamented that hitherto no general attempt has been made to reproduce the old English surplice within our sanctuaries. Independent (*sic*) of possessing a title to our reverence, on account of being a relic of our once Catholic National Church— an incident alone sufficient to demand the restoration of its ancient form—*this vestment comes recommended* to us by its *intrinsic gracefulness*. Its *ample* and *majestic sleeves* and *flowing drapery render it more dignified* and *becoming* than the present winged surplice introduced amongst us from France:"[3] and, I

---

[1] Vestiarium, pp. xxxiii., xxxiv.

[2] Hierurgia, p. 458, note.

[3] In his second edition, 1851, Dr. Rock adds to the above-cited note: "Since the first edition of this work, A.D. 1833, the attempt to bring back

venture to add, more dignified and becoming than any of the various vestments from which *our still*—*Deo gratias*—Catholic National Church has emancipated itself.

With Dr. Rock's unprejudiced testimony to the intrinsic gracefulness, the majesty, dignity, and wholly becoming character of the surplice, and the above-cited authorities for its primitive antiquity, I cannot but agree with the Bishops at the Savoy, that "this habit was ancient, and no habit more suitable than white linen, which resembles purity and beauty, wherein angels have appeared (Rev. xv.), fit for those whom the Scripture calls angels."

But whatever difference of opinion there may be between us on this matter, believe me, none the less, always sincerely yours,

E. B. WHEATLEY BALME.

into use, not only the old English surplice, but many other things belonging to the gone-by times of the true Church in this country, has been made and has eminently succeeded." In our own Church we have sometimes to lament a decadence as to the form of the surplice, on which he could rejoice in a recovery of ancient beauty. A recent fashion among us, is to cut away the dignified length of the old English surplice to a curtness sometimes absolutely ludicrous; and ill-compensated-for by a quasi-feminine display of cassock: while in place of the flowing drapery, which won Dr. Rock's artistic admiration, we have a scanty, flattened, and stiffened form, suggestive of no art but that of a laundress, with smoothing-iron, and unlimited command of Glenfield's Patent Starch.

APPENDIX I.

THE frontispiece to this volume is after De Rossi's plate (tom. ii., tav. vii.,) taken from the crypt of St. Cecilia, in the cemetery of St. Callistus, on the Via Appia. De Rossi, tom. ii. pp. 119-122, concludes from a careful inquiry as to the three figures here seen with names superscribed:—

1. That the Sebastianus here, was the famous St. Sebastian, whose church on the Via Appia was, says Mr. Parker (Catacombs, p. 74), "the centre of the district called 'the Catacombs.'" It is possible that it was the original entrance to all those in that district. For this reason St. Sebastian's was long considered to have been THE CATACOMB, *par eminence*."

Hence, De Rossi supposes the figure of St. Sebastian to have been placed in the centre of the group as the presiding Christian *Genius Loci*, "la cui venerazione veniva di giorno in giorno crescendo e sull' Appia acquistando *il primato*."

The absence of *Sanctus* attached to the name, or *nimbus* to the figure, indicates a date earlier than the beginning of the sixth century, when those distinctions came to be applied to martyrs.

2. The figure with the name Curinus, De Rossi deems to be that of Quirinus, the martyr Bishop of Siscia, in honour of whom Prudentius published, in the first years of the fifth century, a hymn (Peristeph. vii. 1-5):—

> "Insignem meriti virum
> Quirinum placitum Deo
> Urbis mœnia Sisciæ
> Concessum sibi martyrem
> Complexu patrio fovent."

In 378, the Goths devastated Illyria; but about 427, the barbarian hordes were, for a time, driven back; and De Rossi supposes that the Christians took advantage of the interval, to translate the relics of Quirinus to Rome. That they were placed there, on the Via Appia, and in connection with St. Sebastian, appears from William of Malmesbury, "Gesta Regum Angliæ." In his account of the first crusade, under Robert of Normandy, he gives a topographical description of Rome, arranged according to the several gates and roads issuing from them; and gives lists of the catacombs and relics of saints and martyrs to be found near each. Mr. Parker (Catacombs, p. 58) thinks it "nearly certain that William of Malmesbury, in his account of the catacombs, followed an old Itinerary prepared for the use of pilgrims to those shrines; and it is probably taken from a manuscript of the eighth century, preserved at Einsiedlen, which was afterwards used also by Panvinius in the seventeenth century, in his celebrated chapter, 'De Cœmeteriis Urbis Romæ.' The order is the same, and often the same words are used."

From this or other early source, Malmesbury (Gesta Regum, Angliæ, vol. ii. p. 542) writes, "Undecima porta et via dicitur Appia. Ibi *requiescunt sanctus Sebastianus et Quirinus* et olim requieverunt ibi *apostolorum* corpora."

Here, then, we have two saints of our group united, under memories still more sacred, on the Appian way.

3. The third name, though little known, is not far to seek. After mention of some others, Malmesbury continues: "Non longe ecclesia Ceciliæ martyris, et ibi reconditi sunt Stephanus, Sixtus," and others, concluding with "*Policamus martyres*." Here, then, is Polycamus martyr, indicated by the tradition which Malmesbury followed, as lying in the very spot, where our group shows his name superscribed to a figure accompanied by the martyr's palm.

De Rossi thinks that the supposition that the shrine actually contained his relics, is favoured by the position of honour to the right of St. Sebastian, assigned to Polycamus in the group; rather than to Quirinus, who is marked as being a bishop by the tonsure or corona, then distinctive of episcopal rank. Polycamus, on the other hand, he judges not to have been a bishop, both from the absence of the tonsure, and from the position of his name at the end of Malmesbury's list, which is arranged in the order of (1) pope, (2) bishops, (3) inferior clergy or laity.

The name of Polycamus was commemorated by a festal day, the 27th of November, and is recorded in some inscriptions, in conjunction with that of Optatus; which latter also appears alone, in some lists of bishops, whose relics reposed in the cemetery of St. Callistus.

De Rossi's mind has been greatly exercised about the identification of Optatus.[1] By laborious search and piecing together fragments of inscriptions, he is satisfied that Optatus Episcopus Vesceritanus was a Numidian bishop; probably the same to whom St. Augustine addressed his letter, "De Anima" (August. Epist. 190); who seems to have lost his life when the

[1] Roma Sotterranea, II. 222–4.

Vandals from Spain invaded Numidia, A.D. 428, and tortured or put to death Catholic bishops and clergy. In that troublous time, many Catholics, carrying with them the relics of their martyrs, took refuge at Rome, where they were received by Sixtus III. with hospitality to the living, and honour to the dead.

Of Sixtus III., Mr. Parker (Catacombs, p. 21) quotes from Anastasius, xlvi. 65 : " Hic fecit platoniam " (that is, a chapel with the walls lined with marble plates) " in cœmeterio Calixti Via Appia, ubi nomina Episcoporum et martyrum scripsit commemorans."

It is in accordance with this, that De Rossi, from his own investigations, concludes that Polycamus was[1] " un illustre martire compagno o di vita o di morte o di sepoltura ad ottato vescovo ; e fu deposto in une delle crypte appellate ad S. Xistum e ad S. Cœciliam ; " that he was one of the Africans whose relics were brought to Rome about the same time as those of Quirinus from Illyria ; and that the two foreign martyrs were commemorated in the group before us, placed, as it were, under the subterranean hospitality of the native St. Sebastian, by direction of Sixtus III.

It is hardly necessary to point out the resemblance between the vesture of these martyr saints, and the English surplice and stole.

But may we not see here evidence, that it has been by a truly Catholic instinct, under Providential guidance, that the vestment for sacred service in the English Church, has been restored from mediæval varieties, and,—notwithstanding yesterday's imitations of them,—kept, in the main, identical with the vesture attributed to one of the oldest and most venerated of Roman martyrs; to a martyr Bishop from Illyria; with a comrade in the " noble army," from the Africa of St. Augustine ; by a Pontiff distinguished by zeal and liberality for Church ornament;[2] whose own catholicity was stamped by the unanimous approval of his election[3] by east and west, amid the excitement following the Third General Council?

May we not look still higher, and see here a faint earthly image of the " white robes " (Rev. vi. 9–11) " given to the souls under the altar, of them that were slain for the Word of God, and for the testimony which they held; when it was said unto them that they should rest yet for a little season " ?

Is the " gay clothing " of a bridegroom of the eighth or ninth century, (*supra*, p. 161) more suitable than a vesture with such associations as these, for that service which brings man on earth nearest to " all the company of heaven " ?

---

[1] Roma Sotterranea, II. 120. [2] Fleury, Histoire Ecclesiastique, liv. xxvi. c. 48.
[3] Ibid., lxxvi. c. 85.

APPENDIX II.

I have been asked, with reference to the Zurich Letters, whether we have "any letters from old Catholics"? I understand the term to mean Englishmen who, at the time, rejected the English Reformation, and adhered to Rome.

We have statements from that point of view, in the work of Nicholas Sander, D.D., some time Fellow of New College, Oxford, on "The Rise and Growth of the Anglican Schism," continued during the first part of the reign of Elizabeth by Edward Rishton; and published by the latter in 1585.

Mr. Lewis, the English translator of the work, tells us (Introduction, xiv.) that Rishton entered Brasenose College, Oxford, in 1568, and took his B.A. degree in 1572; that in the following year he entered the new seminary at Douai, and from thence was sent to Rheims, to prepare the way for the migration of the seminary thither; that on Easter Eve, 1577, he was ordained priest at Cambrai, and on the second Sunday after Easter said mass for the first time. Rishton, as might be expected, paints Elizabeth in very dark colours, dwelling especially on her hypocrisy. He begins chapter vi. of book iv., which includes her reign, thus (p. 281): "Now as many of these new-fashioned clerks, to avoid superstition, wished to appear in public, and to minister in the church in the ordinary dress of a layman, the Queen issued her orders on the apparel and dress of ecclesiastics. She strictly enjoined the use of a *cope* in the administration of their Eucharist, and of a surplice in the reading of the other prayers, and forbade them to appear abroad without a gown and cap. Even the Bishops must wear a rochet."

Rishton thus entirely supports the writers of the "Zurich Letters," as to the cope and surplice being the only apparel required to be used by priests in divine service under Elizabeth. His testimony is still stronger than theirs, because he was necessarily familiar with the distinctive names and uses of the mediæval vestments, about which such a writer as Bullinger might not be quite clear.

Rishton sets forth Elizabeth's motives thus (p. 283): "The Queen

no vestments as retained, but only cope and surplice.

retained many of the ancient customs and ceremonies, at the persuasion of her ministers, and against the will of the new clergy, partly for the honour and illustration of this new Church, and partly for the sake of persuading her own subjects into the belief that she was not far, or had not gone far, from the Catholic faith. In this matter she behaved with great cunning in her relations with her lovers, suitors, and allies, whether at home or abroad, who were for the most part Catholics. She would raise hopes in them that she might perhaps return to the faith of her predecessors . . . For a long time she *retained the organs, the ecclesiastical chants, the crucifix, copes, candles.*"

If Elizabeth had, in fact, retained the special vestments of the mass, it is inconceivable that Rishton should have left them out of this list. He could hardly have missed the point which it would have given to his denunciations of her hypocrisy, if he could have shown, that she retained the vestments specially appropriated to that service, which she made it an offence, punishable by fine and a year's imprisonment (23 Eliz. c. 1, sect. 4) to celebrate, or even to hear.

Rishton himself felt the weight of her hand. Having been sent over to England with other seminary priests, he was apprehended and sentenced to death, on the same day with the Jesuit Father Campian.[1] In his case, however, the capital sentence was not executed, but he and some twenty others were put on board ship and deported to Boulogne.[2]

[1] Anglican Schism, p. 313, note.   [2] Ibid., p. 328.

APPENDIX III.

Letter by the Rev. T. T. Carter, reprinted by kind permission of Messrs. Skeffington and Son from the Literary Churchman, *Dec. 9, 1881.*

Sir,

No greater boon could be bestowed on the Church of England at this anxious crisis than a happy solution of the difficulties attending the constitution of the Final Court of Appeal in ecclesiastical causes. Mr. Heygate's learning and thoughtfulness would lead one to expect from him suggestions helpful towards such a solution. But I fail to discover any such help in his letter addressed to you, and which appeared in your last issue. He does not seem to have touched the real difficulty. Mr. Heygate says towards the conclusion of his letter, as if settling the question: "Probably litigation would soon entirely collapse, if the Church became her own judge; for after a few test cases it would become clear what she allows and what she forbids; and then all her loyal sons would submit, and if any less loyal refused to obey they would stand alone, or rather, would fall." Good; if all litigants were thus content, or if the Church Courts proper could be let alone to judge finally all causes. But what if one of the parties, feeling that justice has not been done to him by the Church Court, seeks redress in further action? To take, as an illustration, though not a strictly accurate one, the case of a sect. Suppose a Wesleyan minister charged by the members of his congregation with unorthodox doctrine. The Vestry and the Conference condemn him. He appeals to the Court of Queen's Bench. The Queen's Bench examines the trust deeds of the chapel, and decides that his teaching is not at variance with the deeds, and upholds him in his chapelry, temporalities being concerned. What redress have the Wesleyans, except in altering their trust deeds, restating their doctrine, and so guarding themselves against the recurrence of such a wrong? They have, in fact, to seek their remedy in the action of their legislative body.

Our case is similar. A party in a suit in the Church Courts, if he lose his cause, and considers it a failure of justice, appeals to the sovereign to have his case reheard. The cause is sent for this purpose to the Court of Final Appeal, which is not a Church Court proper, like the Arches, any more than it is properly a Civil Court, like the Queen's Bench; *but a court arising out of the relations of Church and State, and judging according to a tacitly understood contract, on the terms of which we hold our property, and our position as the accredited teachers of the nation. The court decides, not whether the Church documents in question are true, but whether the person accused has, or has not, by his teaching or practice, contravened them.* The court is the guardian to the State, on behalf of the subjects of the State, *that the accredited teacher has or has not broken the terms of the assumed contract.* If a wrong is done to the Church by this court through a misrepresentation of its doctrine, its remedy, as in the case of the Wesleyans, lies in the action of the legislative body—our Convocations—by restating the doctrine, and, if necessary, reforming the documents, in which case the State must give its assent to the reformed document, equally as it gave its assent to what had before been accepted. Whether right or wrong, this is our position, and in order to judge fairly of a solution of our difficulties, it is of course important to recognize the fact. It will, of course, strike every one that it would be matter of extremest difficulty for our Convocations at present, in case of a false judgment, to do anything beyond protesting. Still the legislative body alone can alter a Church document in order to make its meaning clearer, or to exclude some erroneous meaning, even as such a body only could originally frame it. To say this, is only to state a difficulty. But it forms one critical part of the problem which has to be solved.

If this be allowed, it is at once evident that the difficulty cannot be met, as Mr. Heygate supposes, by "the Church becoming her own judge," because the question to be determined on appeal, is not what the

Church Court may judge, but what on a rehearing may be decided as to whether the Church Court has kept the terms of the implied contract with the State. If we were disestablished, we should be dependent on a purely Civil Court for maintaining our discipline, and have to guard against wrong being done by false judgments, as in the supposed case of the Wesleyans. Being established, we are similarly dependent on this Court of Final Appeal, and our difficulty is how best to maintain before it what the Church has judged for itself in its own courts.

Again, Mr. Heygate says: "Have those who assert that the present court does not trench upon spiritual authority, because it only interprets documents, ever considered that this is just all that the Church ever does or can do, and that this is her admitted prerogative and duty? The Church not only according to the universal belief and practice of Christendom, but according to Art. XX., has authority in controversies of faith, which authority is exercised in interpreting documents, that is to say, the Scriptures. If another body comes in subsequently and interprets these interpretations, surely it is doing the same thing in principle, and perhaps in effect, on a smaller area, but still the same thing; and surely that second interpretative body should possess not only the same spiritual guarantees, but the same authority as the first did, which authority could only be delegated by the Church, or bestowed apart from on high. No one pretends to the latter. As to the former, the Church has never attempted to delegate her authority in this manner, nor has she power to do so. Were she to attempt such an unfaithful and rash transfer, what validity could it possess?"

This long extract will, I trust, be excused, for it brings out rather remarkably what, with sincerest deference towards the writer, I would venture to characterize as the fallacy which underlies his whole reasoning in this letter. How can a court which the Sovereign power has constituted for the purpose of rehearing causes in which its subjects, wronged as they think in the Church Courts, seek to have justice done them, be viewed as a court to which "the Church has delegated her authority," or as "an interpretative body," "the same in principle," "the same thing," as the body contemplated in the twentieth Article, as "having authority in controversies of faith"? Without at all touching the question as to the necessary conditions for a satisfactory Appeal Court, and having no other object but to point out where the difficulty lies, I venture to think that Mr. Heygate is confusing two distinct things. It is one thing to form creeds and Articles of Faith, to which the twentieth Article refers, and which is the province of the Church Catholic alone derived from Divine authority. It is another thing to judge facts, to test evidence, to decide whether a particular book, *e.g.* coincides or conflicts with a particular Article of Faith, or whether a particular practice is in accordance or not with a particular rubric. A knowledge of Church history, and of the meaning of theological terms, as well as a well-balanced judicial acumen, are much needed for the purpose. But it can hardly be said that a Divine authority is required, "the same principle" as pertains to General Councils. The legislative and judicial functions of the Church are different; and, again, a Church Court proper, and a court which is to see whether the Church Court proper has done justice to all the subjects of the realm in cases where they have a right to be heard, are different. As these bodies differ, so do the qualifications for the members who can fitly compose them differ.

I have little doubt but that as to the end in view my own desire and that of Mr. Heygate is precisely the same. As to the present Court of Appeal, and its late judgments, I also suppose that we are perfectly agreed.

It is only that I am very anxious that the facts of our present position should be properly and clearly stated, and the real causes of our difficulty pointed out, and this has led me thus to express my doubts of his argument.

Whether a court of Bishops only would best fulfil the needed conditions of a sound and trustworthy Appeal Court, is of course fairly open to discussion—it can hardly be said to be essential. If there be lay judges, that they should at least be Churchmen, imbued with the Church's mind, and cognizant of the facts of its history, as well as otherwise qualified to "judge righteous judgment,"—can hardly admit of question among fair-judging persons.

T. T. CARTER.

Clewer, Nov. 28, 1881.

APPENDIX IV.

In Nichols' "Progresses and Public Processions of Queen Elizabeth, among which are interspersed other solemnities," etc., the following solemnities are described as having taken place in 1559:—

"May the 12th, Sunday, the English service began at the Queen's chapel, *which was but four days after the use of it was enacted*, and before it was enjoined to take place by Act of Parliament, which was at St. John Baptist's day. . . .

"September the 5th was a frame set up in St. Paul's quire, of nine stories, for Henry II. of France, who departed this life at Paris in the month of July; and the Queen, according to the custom of princes in shewing honour to each other even at their deaths, appointed his obsequies to be solemnly observed in the chief church of her realm, the Cathedral of St. Paul's, London. The frame was adorned with vallence of sarcenet and black fine fringe, and pencils; and round about the hearse a piece of velvet; all the eight pillars and all the quire hung with black and arms; his hearse garnished with thirty dozen of pencils, and fifteen dozen of arms. . . .

"This magnificent ceremony was performed on the 8th and 9th days of September, beginning the funeral pomp, according to the usage of those times, on the eve of one day, and continuing and finishing it on the morning of the day ensuing. . . .

"The whole expense was the Queen's, which, in all, cost her £789 10s. 10d.

"On Friday, September 8th, when the hearse was solemnly brought into the church, and every man placed, whereas the ancient custom was for one of the heralds to bid aloud the prayer for the soul of the party departed, saying, *Pray for the soul of*, etc., now there was an alteration in the words. For York herald standing at the upper choir door, bad the prayer (as it used to be called, but now more properly the praise) first in English, and after in French, *Benoist soit Eternal*, etc. *Blessed be the King of Eternal*

Glory, who through His divine mercy hath translated the most High Puissant and Victorious Prince, Henry II., late the French King, from this Earthly to his Heavenly Kingdom. Which words he used again at the end of *Benedictus*, and at the end of the service, and again on the morrow, at the times accustomed. The Archbishop of Canterbury in his surplice and doctor's hood on his shoulders, who did execute, began the service, assisted by the bishops of Chichester and Hereford, apparelled as the archbishop, and by two of the prebendaries in their grey amices. And first, certain psalms of praise were sung for the departure of the dead in the faith of Christ, instead, I suppose, of the *Dirige*. After that, one chapter of the Book of Job (perhaps taken out of the *Dirige*), and then certain like psalms. After that was read the fifteenth chapter of the First Epistle to the Corinthians. Which ended, *Magnificat* was sung. And lastly, the latter part of the Evening Prayer. All things ended, they returned in like order as they came (except the banner left in the church) to the great chamber within the bishop's palace. . . .

"Saturday, the 9th of September, about the hour assigned, they met together at the said bishop's palace; and about nine of the clock they proceeded up to the hearse as the day before; and all being placed as before, the three bishops elect IN COPES, and the two prebendaries in grey amices, came forth of the vestry unto the table of administration, and then York herald bad the prayer as before. Then the Communion Office began, and proceeded forward until the offering; when the chief mourner proceeded, the officer of arms, and gentleman usher before him, with his train born, the rest of the mourners following him, but he alone offered, being a piece of gold for the head-penny; and he and others returned to the end of the service. . . .

"The offering finished, the sermon began by the elect of *Hereford* (the elect of *London*, who should have preached, being sick).

". . . After the sermon concluded, they went forward to the Communion: at the time of the reception thereof, the lord chamberlain, the Lord Dacres, and Sir Edward Warner, rose up and went to the table, where, kneeling together with the three bishops, they all six received the Communion; the rest, it seems, of the nobility here present were not yet so well reconciled to the new way of receiving the Sacrament, as to partake at this time of it; all which ended with the other service; which finished, York again bad the prayer, as before. This done, the mourners and others returned to the bishop's palace in order; . . ."

Here, just *four months from the enactment of the Ornaments Rubric*, was a celebration of Holy Communion, forming part of a service of more than usual grandeur and solemnity, under the special direction, and at the cost, of the Royal Authoress of the Rubric. If the vestments were ever to be used with the English service, this certainly was an occasion on which we should expect to find the use.

But it appears that the celebrant, with the epistoler and gospeller, did, in fact, wear NOT VESTMENTS, but COPES.

www.ingramcontent.com/pod-product-compliance
Lightning Source LLC
Chambersburg PA
CBHW020053200426
43197CB00050B/607